CW00855555

/the business of humans

A new working culture where people
and their purpose are more important
than the businesses they run.

O·N·L·E

Copyright © 2021 ONLE Networking

All rights reserved. No part of this publication may be reproduced, distributed, or transmitted in any form or by any means, including photocopying, recording, or other electronic or mechanical methods, without the prior written permission of the publisher, except in the case of brief quotations embodied in critical reviews and certain other non-commercial uses permitted by copyright law.

For permission requests, write to the publisher, addressed "Attention: Permissions Coordinator," at the address below.

Published by Cogiva Ltd.
Kemp House, 152 - 160 City Road, London, EC1V 2NX.

Thoughts from members of ONLE Networking.

www.theonle.network

cont/

/ents

/foreword one.

Writing a book is commonly believed to be the intellectual equivalent of running a marathon - a creative opus that marks a watershed of personal achievement. Writing a book must be arduous, torturous and most importantly, take a long time. Estimates vary, but writing a book should take at least 120 hours and take between six months and one year.

But, is it possible to write a book in one day? After all, if you knew exactly what to write and it was fully formed in your head, the process of committing the words to a page should be dramatically reduced. What if you then brought together people who, with a clear brief, wrote a chapter each and submitted it within ninety minutes? If you could do that, the one-day target is achievable. In fact, one-day drops to 'hours'.

And that's exactly what we did. We brought together the members of ONLE Networking to write about a topic: The Business of Humans. More specifically: can we change the working culture so that people and their aims, preferences, and purpose are more important than the businesses they run? The end result is the book you hold in your hands. It is a book written in hours, and even when we add in the time needed to edit and typeset it, it was indeed conceived, written, edited and finished within one day.

So, while the point of this book is to explore the changing culture of business, it has another very important meaning. This book is about our power as a collective to achieve something that is out of reach for most individuals. It's about why it's important to realise that the physical isolation we've experienced since the Covid crisis changed the world, we were already more fragmented and disparate than ever. Social media can be a force for good, but all too often it feeds a climate of distrust and jealousy. Human beings evolved as tribal beings, but all too often, people are finding themselves alone, arguing online with people who have no interest in learning or changing their opinion.

At ONLE, we believe that people are fundamentally good. And that many others share this view. Contrary to how the media and social platforms portray society, the vast majority of people want to make things better for themselves and their families. But they also want to help friends and strangers and leave the world in a better state that when they found it. And they want to socialise and work with people like them.

We're very proud that within ONLE Networking, we've found those people and continue to find more just like them. We launched ONLE Networking with a simple idea: to become a network that believes people are more important than their business. And certainly more important than profit-for-profit sakes. We're the network for people who like people and to our constant delight, this resonates with exactly the kind of people we like talking to!

We believe this book is just a starting point: our contribution to changing a hierarchy that has made business more important than people. A book cannot reverse this. But a community can.

James & Kelly West, Founders of ONLE Networking.

/foreword two.

Business networking can appear to be a ruthlessly commercial endeavour. You may have heard about, or even experienced, meetings where business professionals pitch and attempt to sell to each other with no interest in the person they are stood in front of. If this is the extent of your business networking knowledge, you'd be forgiven for thinking it's an awful, cynical practice. And in some cases you would be right. Some meetings are like this and I've certainly met my fair share of selfish people whose sole objective is to dish out business cards and sell at people.

But as a business networker of over 20 years, my experience is completely different from this. Here are some of the things I've gained while networking:

Unlimited support. For me and my business. If I have ANY personal or business problem, I know there's someone available to help me. This support is invaluable and potentially incredibly expensive if I had to pay for it.

Knowledge. I have benefited greatly from a few business books, but my most memorable and useful lessons come from people I've met whilst networking.

Reassurance. The business world, as seen through the prism of social media, can look unbelievably shiny. You can be fooled into thinking everyone is perfect. They are not. Meeting amazing people who are just as flawed as you helps keep your feet on the ground.

Lifelong friendships. Really? Really. I've built some of my most treasured friendships at networking. Because ultimately, how do we meet any of our friends? Work? Leisure? If we spend a lot of time engaging with people with shared interests, we build relationships. Networking is a fantastic platform for this.

Business. I've put this last in the list for good reason. Of course, it's important to me to do business whilst networking. But that only happens when I've built the relationships. Many people make the mistake of making this their first (and probably only) priority whilst networking. Not only does this strategy then fail, but they also miss out on the priceless benefits that I've outlined above.

I believe that this book, the story of how it was written and the power of the community that ONLE has built is a fantastic example of what can be achieved if we put people and relationships first. This equation is beautiful because unlike the profit-only approach, everyone benefits. Business owners and their employees are happier, their customers are fulfilled, and the world is positively impacted. And of course, money is made.

I hope this book helps accelerate change and that one day, we'll talk about the business of being humans first and foremost.

Guy Hanson, Publisher, Winchester Resident Magazine.

/foreword three.

Ever since I joined ONLE, one thing has stood out to me and that's the wisdom, passion and experience of the people in the network. I've been to networking groups before. I've been to business groups before, but even after two years, I am still surprised and excited by the brilliance and generosity of the people involved at the heart of ONLE.

And that's the reason behind this project. To take some of that generosity, some of that collective intellect and bottle it. Gather the amazing people of ONLE and see if we can't reach outside the network and share some of the incredible support and joy that I have experienced from this family of entrepreneurs.

It was also an experiment. A demonstration of what is possible even in a very short space of time. When working with high-capacity people that have a lot of irons in a lot of fires, it seemed a lost cause to try to get everyone to find time separately in their busy schedules to write and contribute. So we did it all together, over Zoom, in two hours. We wrote a book. This book that you're holding.

For a brief afternoon, we brought the ONLE network together for a two-hour online meeting and we wrote. We wrote about the human side of business - culture, balance, accountability, trust, fear, etc.. We put our thoughts onto paper and we all spent the time crafting our piece of wisdom to share.

We didn't complete it fully in the two hours. We're not that talented. People went away and finessed their own copy, delivering it a couple of days later, but in the space of 72 hours we managed to draft the contents of a book. We managed to distil the core of the human side of business into 22 essays from some incredibly experienced and generous people.

Simple wisdom, delivered from the heart. We hope you enjoy our experiment and we hope that your business benefits.

Benjamin Drury, The Culture Guy.

O·N·L·E

culture/

/culture

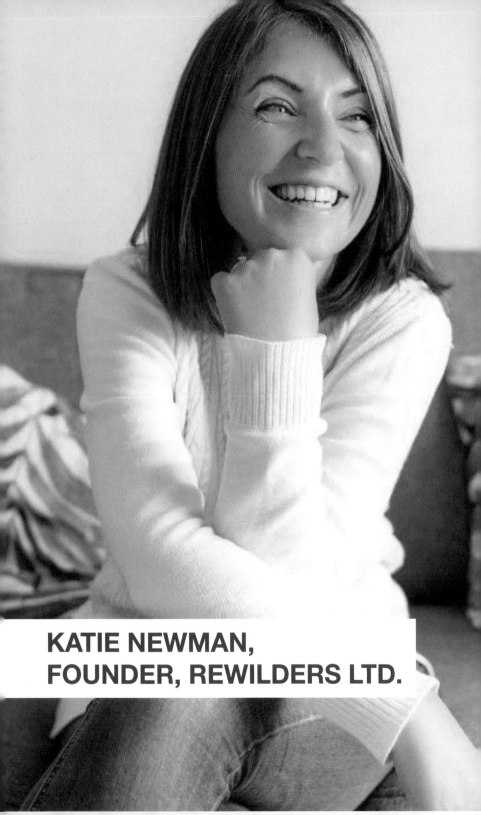

KATIE NEWMAN,
FOUNDER, REWILDERS LTD.

/the value of a value.

Let's start with the basics. What are values? Well, what they're not are some nice sounding, aspirational words which we stick on a website to make us appear caring and ethical to our customers. What they are is behavioural principles that govern how we operate. These are principles that have been formed over many years of experience and learning, and they now sit, firmly rooted in our subconscious, pulling the strings and directing us on how to be, and how to do.

Values are based on 'truths' that we as individuals hold to be self-evident e.g. "the best things occur when you choose the right path, not the easy path". This is one of mine, something I truly believe due to many life experiences that have proved it to be true: choosing to start a new career, ending a relationship that wasn't right, turning down work that my gut told me was wrong. Therefore, because I believe this truth, I value courage. Courage is what I need in order to live my life in accordance with this belief. Courage to choose the right path, and not just to take the easy one.

Every person however has lived a different life and experienced different things. Therefore, it is unsurprising that we all have different 'truths' which we believe, and therefore different values which we hold dear.

As you can imagine, we each hold many, many truths. Therefore, it is unsurprising that when someone is asked to state their values, the list often contains no less than 10 value words: leadership, trust, authenticity, collaboration, simplicity, vulnerability. They all sound great, but which of these truly governs the decisions we make? One of the big mistakes often made is to give someone a list of values to choose from before they've first spent some good time thinking for themselves. The exercise can become reminiscent of hunting for a partner on a dating website. Seeking out all the traits which make up our idea of a perfect human being, rather than appreciating the person we see in front of us.

In order for values to become valuable to us, I would argue you need to get your list down to 3, or if you're feeling brave do a Brene Brown and go for 2. Once you get down to this number of core values, you start to see the true picture of who you are and what makes you uniquely you not the 'you' you want to be, or the 'you' you think everyone else wants to see.

And why is it important to know our core values? Because our core values are our gatekeepers. They create the guard rails within which we operate, and they help us know when we're being congruent with ourselves.

When you look back at the big decisions you've made in life - what career you chose, who your partner is, what made you leave a job - you should either be able to see your core values shining through clearly in your decision making, or else see how their absence took you down the wrong path.

Don't get me wrong, many people quite happily go through life without ever naming their values or even becoming aware of them, they just make what seems like the right call, and then wait to see how things play out, but my view would be, why wait for stuff to go wrong - taking the wrong job, marrying the wrong person - before you figure out what matters to you? If, instead, we all first spend some time understanding the beliefs we hold and the resultant behaviours we hold dear, we're much more likely to get it right first time.

And values aren't just important for our own self-awareness, they're also a crucial tool when it comes to communication and working with others. Understanding someone else's values enables you to better understand them: what's important to them, how they're likely to operate and how you can best work together. Sadly, this isn't language that's often used during team building days. We talk about strengths, preferences, skills, learning styles, but not often do we talk about the fundamental principles we hold to be true which govern how we show up each day. If honesty is really important to you, as your team mate I think I should know that. It's not to say that honesty is not important to me, but I might value other things over honesty- such as efficiency. So knowing what we both value will potentially change how we work together.

And here we reach a really important point. Neither value is right, neither value is wrong, they're just different. And I think this is often where we fall down. We judge each other by our values. If someone states a value, like integrity, which we deem to be very worthy, we often feel guilty that we didn't call that value out for ourselves. Or, if someone states a value, like money, which we deem to be unworthy, they immediately go down in our estimations.

All values are valuable, and in fact we need everyone to have different values in order for us all to work as one whole. If we all only valued harmony and kindness, what would happen to justice and truth?

In order for us to be at our best, as a business or even as a human race, we need everyone to own their values, and to own them with pride. So that when we all show up at the table, we do so as our true selves, bringing all our collective wisdom, experiences and perspectives with us.

Katie Newman is the director and founder of Rewilders Ltd. Katie helps people and businesses to rewild themselves by shedding off their baggage and other people's expectations, so they can come home to who they truly are. She helps them to figure out their purpose, and then develop the courage to bring their unique, talented, squiggly selves to work that makes a difference.

She is a champion of purpose-led business and specialises in supporting those who are out to make the world a better place.

www.rewilders.ltd

She is a professionally trained coach and NLP practitioner, with a corporate and start-up background in marketing, branding and leadership. Katie's twin passions in life are being outside and cheese. She has a secret talent for hula-hooping and spends her weekends working on her vegetable patch and walking in the South Downs with her husband Tim.

/about Katie

O·N·L·E

JAMES WEST, FOUNDER,
ONLE NETWORKING.

/are you working for business or is business working for you?

Why do some people dread work while others relish it?

Answering this question is crucial to making business better for humans.

There are myriad factors defining whether someone enjoys their job: the type of work, their relative level of intelligence and personality type, remuneration, benefits etc. But these factors are specific to the individual, so it's impossible to make a high-level change that will universally alter the outcome.

There are however laws of human nature which define whether someone enjoys what they do that can help solve this challenge. These laws are best explained by thinking about questions a person might ask themselves when considering their job/place of work?

1. Do I fit in? Am I accepted? Do my peers respect and listen to me?

2. Is there any point to what I'm doing? If I work harder, will my contribution make any difference? Do I believe in what I'm doing?

Both of these points are defined by the culture and values of a business. The culture and values of a business signpost what that business believes in, what it is trying to achieve and what it finds acceptable (and unacceptable). This shorthand form of communication is what attracts people who want to be part of the community and culture, either as an employee or a customer. And it is what will define how people answer the questions posed above.

In other words, if a person is part of an entity with culture values that align with theirs, they will feel at home. And this is the starting point for making business better for humans.

Why are connection and purpose so important?

Humans need connection - a feeling of belonging and sharing with like-minded people. Humans also need purpose. These tents of happiness appear in multiple studies and books. For example, Ikigai: The Japanese secret to a long and happy life by Héctor García cites connection and community, and having purpose, as factors that contribute to a person's longevity and happiness. The takeaway from this book is that people who feel part of a community and perform meaningful, valuable work, live longer.

The same conclusion can be drawn from a book that approaches this dynamic from the opposite perspective. Lost Connections by Johann Hari says that the lack of connection and meaningful work are two of the most important factors that contribute to depression.

Therefore, to make business better for humans, we need to make sure that people feel like they belong and that they have a purpose. We are lucky to live in a time when so many of us can choose the type of work we do, rather than being forced to take undesirable employment out of necessity. This is a relatively new development. Ever since the industrial revolution shifted work away from the predominantly agricultural/barter system into a mass production and consumption model, people have lacked this choice. Now, the challenge isn't fighting for the right to choose. It's about guiding people to make the right choices when running their own business. This starts with changing the perception of work. People need to grasp that without connection and purpose, they will continue to look at work as something they have to do, not want to do.

Better for humans, better for humanity

The beauty of this changing the way that people approach and feel about work is that if we make business better for humans, we also make business better for humanity. Businesses with a strong culture are more successful than those with an ill-defined culture. If these businesses then build purpose into their culture, the outcomes can be profound. If for example, a business creates a goal to give to charitable organisations or gives some of its resources to helping a cause, the impact is two-fold.

Firstly, it feeds that sense of purpose of the people involved: the work they do delivers benefits beyond an outcome for the business. Secondly, if the purpose is well-defined, it will have a genuine impact on the world. This creates a virtuous cycle that becomes self-propelling: the positivity creates a stronger sense of belonging in the business, which then leads to better outcomes, which then loops back round.

The business networking spotlight

We see this equation very clearly in business networking. You can almost immediately identify the people who understand their culture and values. They are the people who can neatly position their business proposition. They know who their target market is and how they can help these people. They also know who they don't want to work with and where the boundaries of their business lie.

Their confidence comes from the certainty that having a

cultural compass brings. Their culture defines who they want to work with and for, while their values guide them to make business decisions.

Compare and contrast with the people who attend networking who haven't connected their own beliefs around culture and value with their business. These are the people who present what they do in a very generic way. They are effectively trading their time and knowledge for money. They lack the conviction and passion in what they do because fundamentally, they don't look beyond the time/cash transaction.

The culture of purpose vs the culture of making money

Making money is a purpose of business, but making money in itself doesn't connect with humans emotionally. Yes, some people are driven by money, so while they can absolutely use it to define their purpose, it is guaranteed that their potential customers will not resonate with this.

We connect with culture and values on a very deep level. Think of an organisation or cause that you feel closely affiliated with. You may think of the name and branding. But you'll likely connect with a feeling at the same time. When we align with a culture and its values, we build an emotional tie, a feeling that is far more deep-rooted and valuable than any loyalty scheme or advertising gimmick.

This is the key to understand how to position and market a business. We see many business owners who are clearly unhappy with how their business is developing. They are not quite getting the messaging right. They are battling with social media, trying to write the compelling message or find that magic button that connects them with their audience. And because they fail in this task, they are frustrated and unhappy.

To make business better for humans, we need to help business leaders avoid the trap of trying to position and market their business, and failing time and time again in different ways. They must avoid the shiny lights and immediacy of social media and take a step back. Instead they must document and ultimately embody the culture and values that truly reflect them and their business, not what they think they want to portray. If they do this and then build their messaging and marketing around this authentic culture, they have a chance of creating the 'feeling' that is a magnetic to potential employees who share the culture.

www.theonle.network

James co-founded ONLE Networking with his wife in 2018 after they met at a networking event. He previously worked as a journalist and editor. James' personal experiences also helped him understand the power of networking, connection and community to improve mental health.

/about James

O·N·L·E

GARY MORGAN, BUSINESS &
PERSONAL GROWTH COACH.

/what's the difference?

Motivating staff is a challenge to say the least. Inspiring them is an even bigger challenge. Before we get into overcoming these challenges, let's look at the definitions.

Defining motivation and inspiration

Motivation definition:

> *"The process that initiates, guides and maintains goal-oriented behaviours."*

Inspiration definition:

> *"The process of being mentally stimulated to do or feel something."*

Motivation

Many business leaders will use a variety of ways to motivate their staff. Unfortunately, employees can be motivated by fear just as much as reward. They can be motivated by punishment just as much as praise. It's possible to be annoyed or even angry at the same time. In addition, motivation doesn't have to be accompanied by mental stimulation.

As we can see from above, motivation doesn't always come from positive feelings. I can think of many occasions as a teenager when I was motivated to clean my bedroom. Did I really want to clean my room? No! Did I care if my clothes were in the drawers or on the floor? No! What was my motivation then? Quite simply it was the threat from my Mum that I would get a good hiding if I hadn't cleaned my room properly by the time she came to check.

Inspiration

Inspiration is often sparked by what your employees want to do and a positive vision or outcome. When a person feels inspired, tasks seem effortless. They have feelings of excitement followed by a desire to act straight away. Anything seems possible when an employee feels inspired and they have a great sense of purpose and well-being in the workplace.

As a business leader I believe it is possible to have the intention to motivate employees. Whereas I don't think it's possible to have the intention to inspire employees as I believe that people choose to find us inspirational or not. In fact, some people inspire people that they haven't even met. Serena Williams inspired my young cousin to take up tennis. She has never met Serena, but this doesn't stop her wanting to reach the same high standards in tennis that Serena has set. She dreams of winning the final at Wimbledon and lifting the Venus Rosewater Dish just like her idol Serena has done on seven occasions.

Motivation and Inspiration Activity

Write down the name of someone that has motivated you. Be specific. Perhaps it's a friend, family member, former teacher or even boss. Did they say something that motivated you? Did they perhaps do something that motivated you?

Once you have thought about what they did or said, write those down too.

Now repeat the activity, this time write down the name of someone who has inspired you.

Now that you have written down the individuals who motivated and inspired you, it's now time for you to think about yourself. The thing is, it's incredibly hard to motivate or inspire your employees if you aren't motivated or inspired in the workplace.

You can't pour from an empty vessel

To motivate or potentially inspire others you need to keep your vessel topped up. Like many business owners I work with, I'm sure you are always giving of yourself. Whilst this is an admirable quality, it can take its toll on you if you don't keep filling your vessel.

How to keep your vessel topped up

Below are just some of the ways that you can keep your vessel topped up:

- **Exercise** – This could be as simple as going for a relaxing walk often.
- **Meditation** – Take time to practice this. There are some great apps such as Headspace, Calm and Buddhify that provide guided meditation.
- **Time Management** – Put time in your diary for yourself in the same way as you do for any other important meeting.
- **Family and Friends** – Spend time with people that nourish you. Those people that always make you feel better for spending time with them.

Staff demotivation

According to Forbes, 48% of employees don't like their jobs

and only 30% feel engaged and inspired by their careers.

Here are some reasons why your staff might be feeling demotivated:

- Feeling under-valued
- Working long hours
- Lack of career plan or development opportunities
- Unrealistic workload
- Poor leadership

Ways to motivate
-
- Get to know your employees
- Encourage positivity
- Set realistic goals
- Delegate responsibility
- Give specific feedback on what they're doing well
- Highlight benefits of achievement
- Encourage a good work-life balance
- A good environment and culture
- Say thank you

Get to know your employees

One of my favourite exercises I call the Shield of Knowledge. I often encourage leaders to bring everyone together to take part in this activity. On a flipchart or whiteboard, draw a large shield with a line down the middle. On the left-hand side write the word 'Like' and on the right side the word 'Dislike'. You can then start the process off by writing on the shield one thing in life that you like, and one thing in life that you dislike. Next, invite each employee to take it in turns to list one of their likes and dislikes on the shield. Once everyone has finished, you can use the outcomes to facilitate a discussion about the points that have been written down. By doing this you will be amazed at what you find out, within a very short period of time.

As we said at the outset, motivating staff is a challenge and inspiring them is an even bigger challenge. That said, if you actively apply the above ways to motivate and avoid many of the demotivating factors you will go a long way in having motivated employees and who know, some of them might even find it inspiring.

Key Learning Points:

- Motivation doesn't always come from positive feelings
- Work feels effortless when an employee is truly inspired
- You can't pour from an empty vessel so keep yours topped up
- 48% of employees don't like their job and feel demotivated
- Take the time to get to know your employees and encourage positive communication in the workplace

www.garymorgan.coach

Sales & Leadership Coach, Telephone Communication Expert, Keynote Speaker and Certified Emotional Intelligence Practitioner.

Gary trains Inside Sales, Telesales and Customer Service teams to Sell over the telephone with Integrity.

He also coaches Directors and Business Owners to take their businesses from average to outstanding.

/about Gary

SARAH PHILLIPS, FOUNDER, OCTIMA MARKETING.

/mind the gap.

As a marketer and a writer, I am acutely aware of the power of words – they can inspire, excite, enrage, disappoint, provoke or upset. They can also clarify or confuse. American philosopher, William James said, "Whenever two people meet, there are really six people present. There is each man as he sees himself, each man as the other person sees him, and each man as he really is." Essentially, the complex process from an original thought, how we express it and the way it is interpreted leaves a lot of room for error. In as much as this applies to person-to-person interactions, the same is true in business.

So often businesses start out with the best intentions: there is a clear objective to provide a specific product or service to a suitable target customer. All business activities are to be aligned to supporting this objective. Yet far too often, everyday business activities deviate for one reason or another and a split personality develops. No matter how many people there are in your business, meaning and intent can very quickly become distorted. Before you know it, a simple misinterpretation can evolve into ever-widening gaps of misunderstanding. The left hand has no idea what the right hand is doing. The marketing department is making promises that the customer service team are unable to keep. Management plough ahead believing one thing, when in fact everyone else knows the opposite to be true.

All of this can be incredibly draining for managers, employees and customers. The gaps that develop within our organisation as a result of miscommunication are detrimental to our productivity, the way we feel about our work and inevitably the client experience. After all, who could trust an organisation that says one thing and does another?

In my experience, there are three vital methods to overcome this challenge, all of which must work together: culture, process management, and internal marketing.

Culture

Many more articulate things will have been written on this topic in this book than I can add here, but needless to say, culture is critical. Culture is the shared values and beliefs that bring a team together, the guiding ideals that support every activity that a business does. What do we care about as a business? How does this manifest in our behaviours for our customers? Are we capable of delivering on our promises?

When culture has not been sufficiently defined and shared, the purpose of the business can be distorted. Those who have a sincere emotional investment can quickly become disheartened. This can be particularly poignant when outwardly, the company champions a culture that they do not inwardly identify with. Again, these gaps erode trust inside and out unless they can be bridged.

Process Management

Often the problem here is not a failure to stick to a plan, it is the lack of a plan in the first place. Without clear and defined goals that are accompanied by a set of clear, manageable steps for 'the way things are to be done', ensuring everything and everyone is aligned can be impossible. To ensure any strategies and processes that are developed at the top can be successfully implemented through the business, those responsible for creating departmental strategies should also have some level of input. After all, it is their knowledge and experience that can advise what can and cannot be done on a practical level. This is a truly practical way to demonstrate trust in the team and foster a culture of inclusion.

Once these processes are defined, they shouldn't be locked away in a cupboard or up on a shelf gathering dust. They need to reflect and represent the practicalities of everyday working life. Therefore, every employee, new and existing should be trained and retrained. These processes are the framework that provides reassurance, builds trust and sets expectations.

Internal Marketing

Marketing is not just an outward-facing activity. Marketing defines the way we interpret and address the needs of customers and so touches every part of our business. This is why marketing is not solely the responsibility of the marketing department, pushing out press releases and throwing together 'shouty' adverts that have nothing to do with the rest of the team. For anyone responsible for any part of the customer experience (and let's face it that's everyone), marketing is part of their role.

So why is internal marketing so overlooked? On a practical level, everyone should have the opportunity to contribute to the business' marketing activity – whether it is the knowledge of a product or service that goes into a well-written datasheet, a cross-sell opportunity during a customer support call, or a long-service announcement that shows the world how much you've valued their contribution. We all know the customer is king, but it is the team that makes the magic happen, so they should be the first to know before any announcements go ahead. Some businesses choose to do this with an internal file sharing system or intranet, or perhaps a regular email bulletin or item on the team meeting agenda. Whichever method works for your business, involving every person in the business in your marketing activity closes gaps. By prioritising internal marketing, those awkward pauses when a customer asks about a new product that the sales team didn't even know was on the website can be avoided.

So, before the blame game begins, we need to recognise and rectify the gaps. By gaining a true understanding of every aspect and clearly defining complementary strategies throughout the business, each employee can understand and practically apply to their role. Only then do we stand a chance of communicating to our customers with a unified voice, and see our own organisations as they really are.

www.octima.co.uk

Sarah believes that businesses with purpose deserve to succeed, no matter how big or small. She strives to plan, do and teach marketing that connects with the challenges, motivations, and aspirations of customers.

With 10 years of marketing experience, she currently runs her own marketing agency, striving to show audiences how products and services can solve problems and enhance lives.

/about Sarah

balance/

/balance

KELLY WEST, FOUNDER, ONLE NETWORKING.

/balance and fluidity in life and business.

Is there such a thing as work-life balance?

How many times as an entrepreneur/business leader do you tell yourself off for not helping the kids with their homework, or forgetting to ask, "how did it go?" when your partner gets home from attending an important event? Equally, why is there never enough time to get all those hugely important work tasks completed?

What's the answer? What's the key to a perfect work-life balance? It's simple, there isn't a balance and the less time you spend looking for it, the more time you will have to enjoy life.

Do you love what you do? Are you passionate about your work? Do you have a purpose?

It's taken me many years to realise the answer to all of those questions, and finally I've found the perfect answer to the work-life balance dilemma.

I'm striving to be a mum, a wife, a family member and, by the way, running three successful businesses. How can I spread myself across all of these elements and still do a good job? As I write this, the school has called to say Kennedy has had a fall in the playground. What shall I do? Panic because she could be hurt? Stress because it means I have to drop what I'm doing? In all honesty I will do both. Why? Because both are important to me. And quite frankly, what is wrong with that?

Modern life and the way we work has changed dramatically over the years and the past year in particular has made us refocus and put effort into our number one priorities. But what comes first and when?

Being a parent, you will instinctively put the best interest of your child first. The same goes for being a partner. There will be very few business owners who disagree that their partner comes first. Surely this goes without saying, so why do we struggle with this when we look for a 'balance'? And actually, what is wrong with loving your job and doing the work you do?

As a business owner/entrepreneur, did you start your business with a view to working 9-5 Monday to Friday? If you did, I would question why you didn't just stay employed.

Balance to me means so much more. I have a purpose and that is clear to see for anyone that knows me. I want to make a difference with my business, I want it to change the world and also the lives of the business owners that come into contact with it. Together with my husband, I will run that business to the best of my ability and sometimes (let's face it, most times), this will not fall into the hours of 9-5. Will I beat myself up about this? No. Why? Because my business will enable me to provide for my family and give me the support I need to do this to the level I have set for myself. Not only will it give me great satisfaction to help those external to my bubble, but it will also bring a wealth of support to those in it. This coupled with my clearly defined purpose and goal for the business means I can deal with work or home life as and when I need to.

Easy, right? I can hear what you are thinking - this woman has the perfect life, the easiest kids and a dreamboat husband. Yes of course I do - they are all wonderful! But then you would probably be shocked to learn I am also the mother of a disabled daughter, and surely that makes life hard. It could if I let it and I am sure that every other member of my family could answer in the same way - life is what you make of it. I could have resigned myself to a life of looking after Kennedy and dedicating every waking moment of my life to giving her what she needs, when she needs it, or I could have seen her as being the pure and wonderful girl she is and decided that, for me, life needed to be more than that. It took me a long time to feel comfortable in sharing that with people, but that's how I feel. She brings so much pleasure to our lives, so much humour and so much purity that I really wouldn't have her any other way now. I can't change who she is and why would I? She brings joy and frustration, love and annoyance - but surely that can be said about many relationships? What she does bring is grounding - without Kennedy being the way she is, we would be living life very differently. We wouldn't be as cautious or considered in our decision making. We also wouldn't be up at 5:30am every morning and getting a head start on everyone else!

But this story isn't just about me. It's about you. What life are you living and how can you view it differently? How can you be at peace with 'your lot?' We have a choice: we can choose to constantly battle all the areas of our life that bring us the most challenge, or we can learn to embrace them and make them part of our bigger picture.

Having a child like Kennedy has meant that we now have an even bigger purpose - I can help more children/adults with similar challenges. So much so that we are in the process of setting up a charity dedicated to do this. Would I have done this if I had been given a different angle from the start? No, of course not - out of sight, out of mind. I would have viewed my life, my work and my purpose very differently.

So how can you add purpose to your life and bring 'alignment' to your work-life mix? How can you bring your passion as an entrepreneur into your home life and how can you work on them as a whole, rather than seeing them as separate entities?

ONLE Takeaway: stop putting the importance on 'balance', see the bigger picture and deal with what is in front of you. Set yourself a purpose in life, with a clear goal - include home life in this plan.

www.theonle.network

Prior to setting up ONLE Networking, Kelly worked for a variety of businesses but the common denominator was always networking, which she used to promote her work and build long-term relationships which endues to this day. A natural networker, Kelly loves connecting people and believes that everyone can benefit hugely by focusing on the relationship before the sale.

/about Kelly

**BENJAMIN DRURY,
THE CULTURE GUY.**

/stop balancing and start living.

The word balance is OK when you're talking about nutrition. It's great thing when you're riding a bike: without balance there are only grazed knees and tears. But when it comes to work, I hate the word balance.

When it comes to working, the term balance refers to the ability to separate the different parts of our existence so that we do not overwork and give away any more of our precious time for free than we absolutely have to. It means completely decoupling paid work from the rest of life and never the twain shall meet. It means organisations essentially exchanging an individual's time for an organisation's money. The organisation then has to manage and control that time, making sure people are at their desk working when being paid and they would usually have everyone working at the same time as that is more efficient to manage.

Unfortunately, the exchange time for money is not great for either business or the individual. Not everyone does their best work between 9 am and 5 pm.

A major issue is motivation, particularly when working remotely. There is a fear that people will do the bare minimum of work to get paid and not get fired, whereas in the office they can be watched and "controlled" and made to work hard during office hours for their full allocated time. However, people have a lot of ingenuity when they want to, and if people don't like what they are doing, then they will find ways to slack and get away with it. You can't control people into loving the work and giving their best.

(Daniel Pink's research shows that money is a poor motivator and often reduces productivity and quality, which definitely is not good for business.)

If this paradigm continues when teams are working remotely, then it will have knock-on effects. If people cannot manage their own time and are expected to be at their desk from 9 am to 5 pm, then it has the potential to increase social isolation. Perhaps they have family and other commitments in the evenings and don't get a chance to leave the house because of the strict work expectations. It will also reduce productivity, because under the time-for-money controlled system, people often need to be externally motivated, which is really difficult to do remotely.

Perhaps organisations need to think about fluidity rather than balance - a concept that allows us to make sure we live life enjoying the best of both worlds - being fulfilled in work and fulfilled in life. A way to have enough time to enjoy our family and leisure time, and also feeling like we are doing good, worthwhile work on something that matters.

Perhaps we could treat individuals like adults, not resources. Perhaps we could no longer exchange time for money, but compensate people for value-added or outcomes delivered.

This paradigm frees up the organisation from having to do the management heavy task of accounting for and controlling people's time (the hours they "buy") and they can allow people the freedom to deliver how the individual considers best. Personally I work better from 7 am to 1 pm and then I need a long break, but can do some of my best work between 6 pm and 9 pm. After 9 pm I'm done for though, so my phone and my emails go off.

By giving me the space to manage my own time, an

organisation gets better quality work and I get to connect with people when I want to, solving the mental health issues of isolation. If we allowed a blurring of the edges of work and life, if we expected weekly hours delivered, but do not prescribe the specifics, then individuals working from home, can take a long lunch or have coffee with friends and then work later.

Don't get me wrong, there are times when frameworks are needed when individuals represent organisations and require guidance in the way the organisation wishes to be represented, but often people can be trusted, especially if they have the choice as to when or even whether they do the work or not. I worked with one organisation who implemented unlimited holiday and fully flexible working times and both productivity and revenue went up, because if someone was at their desk, it was their choice, so they chose to do their job well. (People will often surprise you!)

There are also some people that will struggle with the freedom and lack of outside imposed routine. That's OK too. Maybe they need the option of coming into the office to do their best work. It's all about choice and fluidity.

How can organisations move to this new paradigm?

Well the first thing organisations need to do is provide a compelling reason for people to get up, get to work and deliver well. They need to understand and articulate the reason the organisation exists - the 'why' as Simon Sinek calls it - and allow their teams to see the worthwhile, important and impactful work they are doing, so they are internally, personally motivated to bring their best, whether in an office or at their kitchen table. This defined purpose, which should include the organisational values, is what drives people as part of something bigger to bring their whole selves to work.

It allows them to blur the lines between work-life and other areas of life and still be happy and fulfilled, because even their work-life is bringing them meaning.

There are some practical things that organisations should do to make this transition work well:

1. Be clear on both sides (organisation and individual) what the expectations are. When are you absolutely not working? Maybe like me after 9 pm your done, phone and email off. Maybe you put the kids to bed or have dinner with your spouse between 6 pm and 8 pm. Maybe there is a business need to be available on the phone from 9 am to 1 pm every day. Be really clear about what is needed and what is expected.

2. Be clear on the outcomes expected. Are there a certain number of calls that are required each day, each week? Are there meetings that must be attended? Is there a deliverable that is required on a deadline or on site? Do you, as an employee, need access to other people at certain times or intervals?

3. Find ways to communicate that support the business goals and the individual's needs. Does a quick daily catch up work better than two-hour weekly team meetings? Do you need to utilise instant messaging (Slack, FB workplace etc) or does email suit? Find the tools and systems that support the team to get their best work done and keep them engaged with the organisational purpose.

4. Treat people like adults. After you are clear on expectations and have provided the right tools to facilitate the best ways of working, leave the rest up to the individuals. Brian may like to lie in in the morning and work to 10 pm, but he's at every meeting and always delivers on time, why force him to start work at 8 am? Aisha is up and at 'em by 7 every day and by 4 pm she's done for the day, but the work she delivers by lunchtime is

exceptional. When she works late, the outputs are never quite as good. Why force her to work in the evening?

We need to realise that one size does not fit all and that if people have a compelling, worthwhile and fulfilling cause to be part of, they need less managing, less control and CAN be trusted to deliver, whether that's in an office or remotely. Finding balance is about allowing work-life and life-life to co-exist in a fluid harmony. Sometimes that has strict boundaries, sometimes that is lots of give and take. The ultimate aim is not to de-couple, but to find fulfilment, joy and meaning in the whole of life, including our work.

The wider implication of this is that those businesses that are actually doing good and do give their people a compelling "why" will be better suited to survive in the changing economic world of the 21st century and that's good for business, good for society, good for capitalism and good for our shared future.

Benjamin is responsible for England fans singing Swing Low at rugby matches. He's been on Dragon's Den with his invention, Lacemups. He's toured writing, directing and performing with theatre companies.

Professionally he's known as The Culture Guy - the man that makes workplaces awesome. He's a compassionate optimist, always seeking to create a fairer world that works for everyone. He works with extraordinary forward thinking leaders to help build authentic, purpose-led, people-centered organisations fit for the 22nd Century.

He's a husband of one, father of three and he lives at the seaside, mostly watching and coaching rugby.

www.thecultureguy.co.uk

/about Benjamin

O·N·L·E

SAM GRIFFITHS, COACH,
BUILD YOUR MOMENTUM.

/boundaries not balance.

You can't separate life and business. Not if you own a business. If you work for yourself or have built a company, you'll understand how it starts to form a part of your identity, and the inevitable vicious cycle and struggle to 'switch off'.

How can you balance something that, seemingly, has no 'edges'? Forget balance. Think boundaries (and attention). Successful people have clear visions of what they want, what they value, and a path towards whatever it is that means "success" for them. Knowing this sets the scene for the boundaries required to guard their time, space, and energy.

Of course this changes over time as we age and develop ourselves, so it's important to revisit and review this. Boundaries serve to give us control over our lives, and help shape them for the better.

Jeff Bezos, the founder and CEO of Amazon, is famous for not setting early morning meetings. He values quality time with his family, and "likes to potter in the mornings". Even as Amazon grew to the size it has, he has held true to this boundary.

We all have the same time and space to play with, but we choose differently how we use it. Mastering your personal and professional boundaries will go a long way to a healthy and productive life. Your values will help you make key decisions about what boundaries you hold. I've long held the belief that the early morning is the best time for my own headspace, especially to give me time to read, as I have such a curious mind and love to

learn. Reading is my time.
I have two children who typically wake at 7am. If I want that morning reading time bad
enough, I need to get up at 5 or 6am. That leads me to think about what my evening routine
looks like, in order to get to sleep early enough.

Knowing what I value sets the tone for how I construct and lead my life. It's why I believe in autonomy as an integral part of building self care and health. There is no right answer in what time a person should wake, their hours of business, the style of eating they want to follow, or the exercise that is "best". It's personal and unique.

What you do need to question is your results. If you're tired, overwhelmed, have little ability to relax and or control your attention, feeling unfit or overweight, these are results. Ask yourself:

What values do I hold for my health and self care? (Be specific). Do my current boundaries uphold these values? If not, what decisions can I make to change them?

Show me a lean, healthy, happy, productive individual, and I'll show you good boundaries!

thebusinesshealthcoach.co.uk

Sam is the founder of Healthy In Business. His passion for minimalism, love of efficiency, and experience with burnout and mental health challenges in his former years, have enabled him to develop a simple, compassionate, and practical approach to self care for people in business.

/about Sam

SIOBHAN FOX, FOUNDER,
REVEAL MARKETING.

/give yourself permission.

When I started my own business, there were a lot of preconceptions, mental barriers and a giant slice of imposter syndrome that threatened to hold me back. I peered over the edge and thought "I can't do that!"

People that worked for someone else were 'US', whilst people who ran their own businesses were 'THEM'. I could never imagine myself joining that cool crowd of people who worked the hours they wanted to work, earned loads of money and cherry-picked their clients and projects. How wrong was I? I'll tell you: really f***ing wrong!

Not only was I wrong thinking I couldn't do it, but my perception of owning a business was completely wrong, along with the reality of what I needed to do to get there! The thing is, although you absolutely do have the option to earn loads of money, cherry-pick your clients and pick your ideal work hours, that shit doesn't happen overnight. It takes time, patience, hard work and an appreciation that once you start a business, your life and your work are no longer two separate things.

The main driver for starting my business was to find a better balance of working and spending time with my little boy. Working 5 days a week felt wrong, but I also knew I couldn't be a stay-at-home mum (lockdown proved me right on that one). So, with my son raising hell at nursery 3 days a week, I have spent the last 18 months building a successful business working a maximum of 25 hours a week. And, I actually did it!

So, I am here to tell you that if you spend your time on the right things, all these long days and nights hustling to get a new business off the ground are not required. Nor should they be! The real trick is, when you figure out the work-life flow that works for you, you'll be happier, more fulfilled and you will very likely earn more money than ever before.

So where do you start?

For me, it's about humanising your vision. Don't just paint a picture of what your ideal business could look like, paint a vision of what your life will look like alongside it. As well as thinking about how many hours you'd like to spend working, think about how many hours you'd like to spend on your hobbies, with your family, going for walks, cooking, reading, staring out of the window and so on. Once you flesh out the vision of your life in its entirety, it allows you to step back and see what's really important to you. From there, you can build a business in a way that supports your life, rather than the other way around.

Besides, isn't that why you wanted to jump into self-employment in the first place?

Don't get me wrong, the myths still abide. I see it a lot: 80-hour weeks, hard graft and missed family time worn as some kind of badge of honour alongside a successful business. For me, it's the people that tell me they've grown their business whilst being on maternity leave, or whilst training for a marathon, that have inspired me to chase after the work-life flow that works for me. Aren't they the real winners?

OK, so how does it work in practice? I'll be honest: it ain't easy! I deliver all my client work over Zoom, I start my days at 10am, insist on a lunch break, and sometimes even make use of the child-free time to meet friends for coffee or enjoy a well-earned Netflix binge. But, do you know how long it's taken me to give myself permission to do these things? At least a year, no word of a lie. I've had to unpack nearly 20 years of 40-plus-hour working weeks, clock-watching, boss-pleasing and 9-5 life. The sad thing about all that corporate baggage is that it is evidence of never being appreciated as a whole human being.

So much of office life can just be about showing up, sitting at your desk for the allocated amount of time and keeping your personal life out of sight. The even sadder thing is, a lot of employers miss a trick. All the evidence says that the more you treat your employees like human beings, the happier they'll be and the better your output will be as a business! Quite apart from being the right thing to do on a human level, it's also better for profit margins. Who'd have thought it?

Herein lies the big lesson for you, my entrepreneurial friend: the fastest, easiest most enjoyable way for you to grow a successful business is to look after yourself. Recognise, appreciate and nurture all the sides of yourself and you will be on the fast-track to the life you have always dreamed of.

When all is said and done, what do you want to be able to say to your grandchildren? That you worked like a dog all your life? Or you spent some lovely time walking the dog?

revealmarketinguk.com

Siobhan is a Marketing Strategist, mum, wife, cheese lover and aspiring author. Following a 20-year career working for corporates and agencies, she now owns her own marketing business.

Living in Winchester with her husband, son and judgemental cat, she enjoys writing, drinking coffee, reading, swearing and making people laugh.

/about Siobhan

O·N·L·E

**FREDERIKE HARMS,
BUSINESS STRATEGIST.**

/the advantage of not fitting in.

My grandad and even my dad would often have a beer for breakfast.

No, they weren't alcoholics, but they were bakers. I'm a proud baker's daughter and, not to make you jealous, I could walk into the shop and take whatever I wanted, whenever I wanted, without paying.

Back to the beer though, because my grandpa and dad both worked through the night, our breakfast would be their dinner before they'd go to bed. Of course, there didn't seem to be anything wrong with that, until my friends started to spend the night and it caused some raised eyebrows at breakfast.

Then, when I had to move on from primary school (in Germany), my parents decided to send me to a private grammar school not far from where we lived.

My parents weren't rich, they had their own bakery business with two shops and some restaurants, and hostels as customers at the time, but the cost of the school was huge considering the money they made. They didn't make that choice because they thought they were something better, but because they didn't think the public school had a good reputation and wouldn't help me reach my full potential. To make sure I got the best education possible, they gave up holidays and other luxuries to pay for my schooling instead.

My 10-year old self was devastated because ALL of my friends were going to a different school and I was the only one left out.

Being at a private boarding school, as a day student, I was also the only person in my year that had to get a job as soon as I was old enough. I spent at least 3 nights and one day a week waitressing at an American Restaurant and Bar, earning money to pay for my first car, coach trips to Paris with my friends and all the makeup you'd possibly need as an 18-year-old (which is a lot to be fair).

I was often tired and I didn't have as much time as my friends to study for my A-levels.

The thing is, at the time, I always hated standing out. I wanted to be like my friends and do the things they did. I was frustrated with having to work and not having as much time to study. I couldn't believe my parents would 'hate' me so much that they would send me to a different school.

As entrepreneurs in today's world, we often feel the same. We see the success stories of those "overnight successes". We see that post by the lady in the membership who just grew her Facebook group by 300% in two days. We hear about the guy who launched his first course and made over $60k.

Sometimes, this spurs us on and fills us with ideas, but often, this makes us wonder why we can't have those blinkin' successes and what secret talent we're missing. We wish we'd have had that idea. We wish we were more like them and that we'd fit in.

"Why is everyone doing so much better than I am?"

Thing is, they're not. We're buying courses and books, joining groups and memberships to find out what to do to make our business a success. What do we forget? That we're all different and that one thing that brings in millions for someone, may not be the right fit for us.

Running a successful business is not about fitting in and doing what everyone else is doing. It's about doing what works for you, what is in line with your offering and what works for your lifestyle. There is no 5 pm cut off for entrepreneurs, so you need to design an entrepreneurial life in harmony. You won't mind answering emails on a Saturday morning if it's because you took Wednesday off to spend the day with your partner for his birthday and you love what you do.

At the same time, you want a business that can support you even if you become a homeschooling teacher overnight and have to rearrange your 3-bed end-of-terrace cottage to fit in two offices and three school desks.

While the age of the internet, and social media especially, encourage constant comparison which can be inspiring. It can also leave us overwhelmed and exhausted. Instead, you should get clear on the life you want the business to support: working three days a week rather than seven; meeting clients in beautiful hotel lobbies rather than functional, beige rooms in a boxy building by the airport; a retreat in Florence rather than Birmingham, and you should identify your zone of genius - that sweet spot of what you're good at and what you're passionate about, that would make you get out of bed excited.

All the while understanding that there's nothing as certain as change, so be forgiving about shifting direction. Your business model will likely adapt as your priorities and circumstances evolve.

Building YOUR business is exciting. Make sure it's everything you want it to be.

www.frederikeharms.com

Frederike Harms is a Business strategist and coach. Her mission? To help you start and build a 6-figure business while working 9 - 5. You'll never find her spouting a motivational speech and then disappearing into the ether. She likes to get her hands dirty with crystal clear plans and strategic goals. She's German, so it's a genetic thing, but she's also bossed it as a Project and Change Manager for global players like Starbucks, Unilever and Mercedes for over 15 years.

/about Frederike

O·N·L·E

**SEAN TOOMER,
REBEL ACCOUNTANT.**

/blood, sweat and tears.

Guaranteed you've heard that saying before. In my opinion, it's overused, used out of context and used by people who are not entitled to use it.

Just because you run a small business, and you're working 12-hour days, doesn't mean your blood, sweat and tears have gone into that business. You're a business owner; that's what you should be doing.

Just recently I was chatting to a new client. We 'clicked' quite quickly; she was obviously our ideal client, and I'd go as far as to say we were the perfect accountants for her. She used this phrase, and for once, I actually thought, 'you know what, you HAVE put your blood sweat and tears into this business'.

- She'd cried herself to sleep because she couldn't afford the rent anymore and had to go mobile.
- She'd had many DIY disasters, including breaking her wrist, doing things she wasn't 'qualified' to do at all, but had to be done.
- She spent many nights and weekends sweating physically when a normal person would have quit, taken a shower and ordered a big fat pizza.

Nothing can stop an actual, proper 'committed' small business owner. They are like a juggernaut and once they've built momentum there is no such thing as an immovable object.

F*** you Newton and your third law.

I was once having a conversation with a small business owner, and we were talking about keyman insurance. He told me he didn't need it, because nothing would stop him getting done what needed to get done.

Broken leg? The most committed can, and will, still operate a laptop.

Chopped off hands? Have someone type for you, or use a dictaphone or some other app that can help (a committed business owner would find one).

Suffering severe back pain and can only lay down? Make a ridiculous looking, yet still functional desk on wheels to go over your bed so you can still keep working, whilst laying down.

The last one is true. It was just after the first Covid-19 lockdown in the UK and I was in agony with severe back pain. My job requires me to sit at a desk and work on a computer, and what caused the most pain was sitting at a desk.

'You're f***ed' most would think.

The biggest motivator for me, quite selfishly (and I'm not afraid to admit this), wasn't about being there for clients, being there for them, at a time they so desperately needed my help and advice on what they could claim, what the hell 'furlough' meant, and how their business was going to get through this. It was the fact that if I wasn't there for clients, this would hinder our growth, hinder our reputation, and ruin everything I'd been so committed to building over the last 10 years.

This is exactly what commitment looks like.

But it's not just physical barriers. It can be mental too. Especially if you're doing something that is a bit different. The commitment small business owners are required to have to block out the negative, the 'haters' and the jealous, spiteful d**kheads is phenomenal.

We're doing something very different, and it's required levels of commitment from myself that I never knew I had (proven by the fact that I can't give up smoking no matter how hard I try – perhaps because I REALLY want to!). I've been called a 'clown', been told I 'don't look old enough to have left school' and accused of being 'unqualified', all because we took a different approach to accountancy that hasn't been tried before.

I've been right alongside a business owner's journey where they left a comfortable, well paid job, put all their savings into a business, then borrowed, then borrowed some more to get their idea moving, all the while, everyone around them is telling them it's clearly not working (including me), but they just can't be told any differently. Not 'won't' be told any differently. 'Can't' be told any differently.

They went on to be a success (this would be a crap story if they didn't, huh?).

Commitment is crying (screaming) inside, feeling like everyone thinks you're a dumbass, yet having the audacity to smile and whisper 'f***-you' to anyone who tells you differently, because nothing will waiver your faith.

This is what commitment feels like. 'Commitment' for small business owners is having the absolute, unequivocal belief in what you're doing is the right thing, it's what your chosen market is so desperately crying out for, and above all else not letting anything, anything stop you on your mission to do just that.

> **'I am the greatest. I said that even before I knew I was'.**
>
> Muhammad Ali.

This is what commitment sounds like.

Sean Toomer is the owner, founder and MD of Diverso Accountants, a unique innovative company working exclusively with small businesses.

www.wearediverso.com

Diverso provides not only accounting, but an extensive package of free business support and advice all included in a monthly subscription fee – really helping SMEs manage cash-flow. As Sean says, he isn't looking to change the world, just looking to change it for small businesses.

/about Sean

trust/

/trust

SIMON TUCKER,
PROFITABLE CONVERSATIONS.

/trust me I'm a salesman.

Trust is something we do or we don't.

I am a person who trusts everyone I meet, until they break that trust. I am open to everyone's opinions, views, beliefs. Trust is important for personal relationships, families, communities and business to function well.

In their book, 'The Trusted Advisor', Maister, Galford and Green, came up with the concept that trust could be measured in some way. To explain that they used an equation:

$$T = C + D + R$$

T = Trust – C = Credibility – D = Dependability - R = Relationship

Essentially, in business terms, this can translate to the fact that you can build trust, over time, with your clients.

For example, my credibility in business will come through my qualifications and experience – i.e. a medical practitioner gains instant trust with patients due to the fact that we believe they have been to medical school and are qualified.

My dependability comes from doing what I say I will do for the customer. I deliver on my promises – i.e. if I say I will send a sample, I do. When it arrives with the client, their trust in me increases a little more.

The relationship is the part that takes a lot more time to develop. Sometimes relationships take years to build, but as long as I continue to treat the client as a person and, perhaps, show more interest in them than just the pure business we do, then the relationship will grow and blossom.

However, there is a caveat to this relationship. Steve Chalke added to the equation:

$$T = C + D + (R/S)$$

What he means by adding the (R/S) is that relationships are often spoilt by 'Self-Interest'. If one person feels that the other is only developing the relationship for what they themselves can get from it, then the trust is diminished by that self-interest.

Now that applies in any relationship, but in business, the biggest driver of suspicion of self-interest is money. If the customer believes that you are only into building a relationship with them because it will make you money, then trust in you, your product and your services is very much diminished.

Sadly, where this hurts businesses most is in sales and marketing. How many potential customers are put off by a marketing message that says 'Me' not 'You'? How many customers won't even consider trusting a salesperson because they believe that they are only into the relationship for the commission they can earn?

The image of sales is particularly tarnished by bad or even illegal selling practices. Let us just take the example of Payment Protection Insurance. What did that scandal do to the trust we have with banks?

It is vital, in my opinion, that as business people we focus on the customer, not ourselves. If our purpose is to provide a useful product or service, then let's focus 100% of our effort in building and delivering on that purpose. Because, if we do, the money will flow. It goes without saying that if we build something useful, people will buy it!

The simplest way to start building a relationship with another person is to show genuine interest in them. How do we do this? We ask open questions, about them, their circumstances, their business, their needs, their wants, their desires and their ambitions.

Rapport starts with the first conversation.

> **Rapport (n) - If two people or groups have a rapport, they have a good relationship in which they are able to understand each other's ideas or feelings very well.**
>
> Collins Dictionary

Just about every sales trainer on the planet will tell you that you need to build rapport with customers. Well, guess what? Rapport starts with the first conversation you or your business ever has with a potential customer. Rapport is about them, not you. Rapport is the very start of any relationship - business or personal.

If we as business owners want to genuinely build a long-term, trusting relationship with our customers, everyone who ever communicates with a customer must be skilled in building rapport by asking great questions.

Equally, the importance of true, deep relationships with our staff and colleagues needs the same application of the trust equation. If those relationships, from either side, are just about money, they will be forever shallow.

Good communication in relationships can be enhanced by simply asking good questions.

I keep six honest serving-men
(They taught me all I knew);
Their names are What and Why and When
And How and Where and Who.

The Elephants Child, Rudyard Kipling

Simon Tucker is the owner of Profitable Conversation, a salesconsultancy, coaching and training business.

Simon is an experienced business builder and a people developer. He started by selling toothbrushes and finished his employed career as European Sales & Marketing Director. He has worked and lived in the UK, USA and Switzerland.

profitableconversation.com

In 2005, Simon and three colleagues built Medenta Finance from zero to over £24million per year. In 2011, Medenta was sold to Practice Plan.

Having spent more than 40 years working in business, Simon still says that his biggest moment was appearing on the BBC Children's programme, "Why don't you…" in 1973.

/about Simon

JOANNE BONNETT,
ARBONNE.

/a matter of trust.

I've got your back. You can count on me. I'll be there for you.

I'll be there for you – how many of us are already humming the 'Friends' theme tune, but what does it look like to be there for someone in business (or in life), in a way that makes a difference, grows trust and builds an emotional bank account to support yourself and others in good times and bad?

It's easy to be there when time, money and resources are plentiful. When the trends are all going your way, the livin' is easy and the cotton is high. It's quite a different tune though, when our cups are empty, money's too tight to mention and the long and winding road ahead seems lonely and full of obstacles.

Most people in business will be familiar with times of conflict, challenge, change and tough decisions to be made – and I'm an optimist so I'm expecting there to be even more times of anticipation, celebrations, breakthroughs and growth. I firmly believe showing up ready to add value, whatever the circumstances, is where the joy breaks through.

So, in a world where there are increasingly blurred lines rather than clear borders between work and pleasure, colleagues and friends, potential clients and networking buddies, who do we trust and why? More of our business and social interactions are taking place via our screens and from inside our homes. Potential customers now have a window into our private spaces and if that's who sees us on a not-so-bright-and breezy-morning, can we trust them and ourselves to be vulnerable and have a real conversation?

I love an acronym, so here are some points I've observed that help me check in with myself and others:

- **T – TIME.** Our most precious resource, so being prepared to be present to listen to an idea, talk through a challenge, offer support (we all need cheerleaders), show up or collaborate will always be valued. Time after time after time.

- **R – RESPECT.** Find out what that means to me or to you. And that's the point. We may think and behave differently, but take a step back and look for the good in people, discover common ground and know that so much of life's beauty comes when colours on the opposite side of the colour wheel (think yellow and blue, sun and sky) are seen side by side and balance each other perfectly.

- **U – UNIQUELY YOU.** It's (not) all about you, but it is about you being you. Wouldn't life be dull if we all agreed, spoke the same, dressed the same, responded the same? Comparison is the thief of joy, so if you want to feel good about yourself, be yourself – and that gives others permission to be themselves too.

- **S – SHARE.** Are you a giver or a taker? Showing personal vulnerability isn't easy (and there are appropriate levels here) but there's enormous strength in revealing weakness where it is relevant. Beware the overshare, but trust is a two-way game, and remember to keep confidences close to your heart. This also applies to sharing sound advice, connections and supporting others by choosing and using their products and services where you can.

- **T – TREASURE.** Where your treasure is, your heart and energy will flow. What do you treasure? Others will see it in you and it will be reflected back. Whether it's relationships, connections making a difference, being values-driven or an interest in others, be genuine. Imagine everyone has a sign on their head saying 'make me feel important'. How good would it feel to know there's one on your head too? Now replace that with a note that has £$£$£$ signs. Not such a good feeling. Yes, business is ultimately about profit but we are human beings before we are human doings, so treasure who people are, not just what they can do for you.

When we keep a positive balance with the T-R-U-S-T points, the feel good factor starts to flow and, as well as helping others, we boost our own self esteem and emotional resilience. Our emotional bank account is not only topped up by the good things that happen to us, but also by the way we serve and show up for others. The law of reciprocity in action shows that when we prove ourselves to be trustworthy, people respond to us in the same way.

I've always trusted other people quickly and there are only a few times in life that it's caught me out! A kind friend once said that those who trust easily are easy to trust because it's simply an expectation. What if we dare to truly believe the world is a beautiful place filled with kind, thoughtful, helpful, trustworthy people? If we're unlucky enough to come across someone who doesn't fit that description once in a while, that's the time to draw on our emotional reserves. It hurts at the time, but it's better than living in a permanent state of mistrust.

Is it naïve to think that in the same way we are embracing hybrid working, where our home becomes our office and 9 to 5 is history, we can build long-term, trusted relationships in business as well as in our personal life? I certainly believe all our emotional accounts will spend more time in credit if we do.

And I've got a feeling that will only be a good thing for everyone.

www.arbonne.com

Joanne Bonnett is a positive, curious people-person who is passionate about helping others to live well (and age well!). With a background in corporate marketing, she now has a thriving online health and wellness business, is a values-driven leadership coach and mentor and if she isn't reading or learning, she may well be singing!

/about Joanne

accountability/

/accountability

GUY HANSON,
PUBLISHER.

/accountability.

Having a business idea is only the beginning, but is it the right idea?

Whether you are starting out for the first time or are stepping off the corporate hamster wheel to create a new work-life balance, an initial idea needs to be scrutinised before you make any plans.

When I chose to start my own publishing business in 2016, it was a combination of being disillusioned with my job and wanting to control my own destiny to benefit my family. The first thing that I realised was that having been in the corporate publishing world for over 40 years I had always directed sales teams, editors, design and production staff and a distribution and print process – now it was about having to fill all these roles alone, and answer only to myself. I had to become accountable for my own results from a standing start.

It was daunting from day one but I had taken the time to make two very important decisions before I began. It wasn't a case of head down and struggle on without a plan. More of a process of deciding how I wanted to approach my business and having a goal to achieve to keep me focused.

Step 1: The book 'Good to Great' by Jim Collins taught me The Hedgehog Concept. This looks at an ancient Greek parable advising that people are either hedgehogs or foxes and transfers it into business thinking. Essentially, the fox knows many ways to try to trap a hedgehog, but a hedgehog knows just one thing – how to stay safe and outwit the fox. By focusing on just three things this, concept provides a 'sweet spot' where your business should be focused. It truly gave me the clarity to concentrate on one thing and not to be distracted.

Firstly, what are you passionate about? Secondly, what can you be the best at doing? Finally, what drives your economic engine? (e.g. what makes you money?)

By really thinking about these three things (not overnight), you should be best placed to know how to position your business. For me, I am passionate about print, can honestly be the best local print media, and the amount of revenue I create per advertising page defines how much money I make. This gave me accountability and would ultimately determine the results I achieved. For example, I know little about social media, I am old school, and therefore I decided not to embrace it and do it badly, but to concentrate purely on my print offering. That's the 'hedgehog' in me, doing only what I do best whilst other publishers became distracted by chasing 'other' revenues that were, and still are, incredibly difficult to realise in the publishing world, both locally and nationally. I really cannot recommend the 'hedgehog concept' enough. It truly drove my business forward with a focus and all I needed was a goal to link it too.

Step 2: How was I going to come up with a goal? My entire corporate career was built around motivating others to achieve results that rewarded everyone uniquely and encouraging teamwork for a common purpose, but now it was just me.

The principle was the same though and I immediately turned again to Jim Collins, and another of his works Built To Last. This book had taught me years before how to motivate others through producing a 'BHAG', and it was time to put it into practice for me!

A 'BHAG' is simply a big, hairy, audacious goal. This is not simply a target, not something easily achieved, but something so stretching that it seems virtually impossible at the time of its conception. It's all about having the right people on board who think the same way and are all moving towards achieving the BHAG as one. If someone didn't believe it was possible, they had to be removed from the team, something I was never shy about doing in my own teams for the good of everyone else involved. As Jim Collins puts it 'having the right people on the bus in the right seats'.

The greatest 'BHAG' example that you can relate to is US President Kennedy, who in late 1962 told everyone that by the end of the decade, they would put 'a man on the moon and bring him safely back'. What a goal. How outlandish that would have seemed back then. How very audacious to even think up such a thing!

My BHAG was clear to me - within 5 years I wanted my wife to be able to stop work and for me to work when I wanted to work, with the people I wanted to work with. These two statements were highly visible everywhere I worked.

This gave me focus every day. It wasn't an idea hidden away in a drawer and forgotten about. (Remember your own job appraisals, in most cases a simple box ticking corporate exercise.) This was my daily motivation. I focused back regularly on my hedgehog concept, deepened my passion, became the best I could be in my field and consistently grew my revenues with no additional cost base.

Today, just 4 years later, I have achieved both of those goals.

It was by no means easy. It was never meant to be. It took a lot of thought, work and concentration on not being distracted by others, going off on a tangent to try other things too. No, I knew which direction I was heading and was relentless in pursuing it. My life is now just as I saw it.

As you begin your journey, I seriously recommend you seek out the work of Jim Collins (Hedgehog Concept and BHAG are both found on You Tube). Without that focus and drive, I would not have achieved the perfect work-life balance that I so wanted.

Your only real competition is looking back at you from the mirror.

residentmagazine.com

I have been involved in the
world of publishing, both
local and national print media
for over 40 years. Print is
my passion. Today, I run my
own publication and built my
business to realise the
work/life balance that I chose
to achieve.

/about Guy

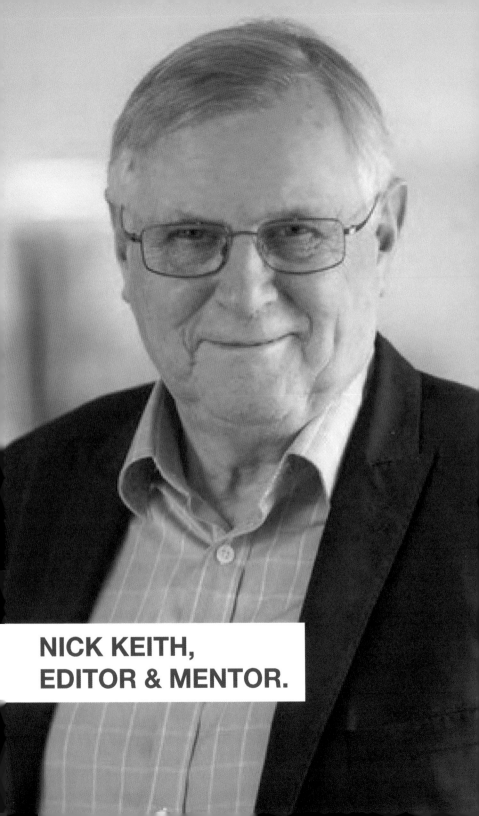

**NICK KEITH,
EDITOR & MENTOR.**

/respond and deliver.

Accountability and results are two vital elements of business. But what do they mean?

Accountability carries a sense of responsibility, which, in turn, means 'being able to respond'. Stephen R Covey sums it up: 'Accountability breeds response-ability.' Results embody outcomes, consequences, effects and even decisions, as well as sums, totals and all the financial considerations of selling a product or service. Accountability and results go hand in hand. As the old song says, "You can't have one without the other."

Let's start with accountability. "Accountability is the glue that ties commitment to the result," according to Bob Proctor, speaker and author of recent best-selling business books 'The ABC of Success' and 'It's not about the money'.

Fresh ideas are coming into the vocabulary and practice of business and, it is hoped, they will grow and expand in the new post-pandemic world of work. For me, accountability requires openness and the ability to respond to challenge. The terms openness, vulnerability and wholeheartedness are urged on people in business and in life by Brené Brown, research professor at the University of Houston, who covers social issues.

When she was researching connection, she heard stories of disconnection from the hundreds and thousands of people she interviewed. They felt disconnected and of no account, not worthy. It is hard to feel responsible and accountable if you are not being heard. Her TED talk on 'the power of vulnerability' has now been viewed by more than 50 million people worldwide.

In the workplace we need the opportunity to be open and accountable for our actions and our thoughts or feelings. This is all part of the communication cycle and, of course, accountability needs to show up to ensure secure and productive environments. Accountability also means that people need to stand up to questions and challenges about their performance; to give a clear account of what they have done, or not done, and why, and how that has impacted on outcomes, decisions and performance. Accountability can be presented and tested through written reports and physical meetings. The reports will often lead to meetings.

Results are very important but they have their nuances. Many business people see the term as having an overriding financial flavour. However, good financial results are much harder to achieve without dedication to clear communications, discussions, decisions and their consequences.

Results are much more than financial achievement: the satisfaction of customers is a result; the satisfaction of staff, so that they work smarter to achieve better outcomes, is a result. Results can be short-term, but, if they are long-term, that is in the best interests of the company and the staff. Other questions about accountability include: What are the drivers? Who or what are people accountable to? Who is involved in the process of setting up the objectives? How often does that happen? Who is responsible?

My older half-brother, Patrick Barbour (now a lively 86) founded and ran two highly successful publicly quoted companies from the 60s. Barbour Index provided information services to the construction, health, safety and environment sectors – to "improve decision-making, understand complex information areas, reduce risk, manage projects, specify products and choose suppliers."

Initially, this service was provided through the Barbour Compendium, a large printed encyclopedia of building materials which architects and the construction industry bought for thousands of pounds each year. In time the compendium was saved into micro-fiche format, and then developed digitally. And the service expanded into other sectors. The company was acquired by Hachette, the French publishers, when he retired.

To help achieve accountability and results in Barbour Index, Patrick had an open-plan office on one floor where he had a room at one end with his door always open. He recalls how he spent some 20 years perfecting a specific way to set up an annual accountability framework.

- Every person sets their own objectives and plans (O & P) within the organisation's or department's objectives. There are five main ones, at every level down to individual.
- The organisation establishes the overall long-term dreams and objectives. Within these, teams and individuals set their own.
- These are agreed with managers, amalgamated up and reviewed monthly.
- Managers are responsible for looking after their staff.
- The organisation's O & P need to cover no more than two pages, because each level adds key points to plans.
- The objectives need to be measurable, but that is part of the plan.

The aim is to get people to own their responsibilities. So, if they set their own objectives and plans, they are likely to drive themselves to achieve them. In several ventures, Patrick has helped me write business plans. He does not believe that companies need to be hidebound to their business plan for the sake of accountability. And business plans should occupy a maximum of two sides of A4, with one of the 3 or 4 aims being, "To have fun".

In a long career in the media, publishing books and magazines, and marketing, I have always adhered to these principles and not been a slave to hard-wired results and accountability. I have enjoyed all my various jobs, and companies where I have worked, by being accountable both upstream and downstream in these businesses.

Vince Lombardi, the revered American football coach, has said that "The achievements of an organisation are the results of the combined efforts of each individual." And business leader Jack Welch, legendary CEO of General Electric, has praised 'boundary-less' organisations, where everyone from the janitor and beyond has a voice and is heard. He wrote in his book Winning:

> **"When you were made a leader you weren't given a crown, you were given the responsibility to bring out the best in others."**

In other words, accountability is partly personal, while results are achieved collectively. People can only deliver results if they are able to respond to their circumstances.

bestbusinessenglish.com

Nick Keith is an expert editor of business books, copywriter and author. A journalist and former sports editor of The Times, he was founder / CEO of 2 separate publishing businesses in books and B2B magazines, and director of a marketing company.

/about Nick

JEN TODD, BOOKKEEPER, SILKBOW GROUP.

/the gym.

As a bookkeeper, this may seem an obvious choice for me to write about. However, my story is not about numbers as that could be deemed to be very boring, but it's about holding yourself accountable and seeing the results.

My story is about someone we will call Jin, who finds herself struggling to get up and down off the floor and having her fitness levels drop. This no doubt happens to everyone, but Jin used to be very fit and healthy and now is unhappy about the struggles.

Whilst sitting in a business network meeting she listens to a chap that talks about getting people fitter without going to a gym, changing their mindset and ultimately improving their life. Jin sees this as a possible way to help her. She books to see this chap (who we will call Dave) and have an initial chat. The meeting goes well, but Jin decides that she won't do anything about it at the moment as she can surely do these things herself.

Three months go by and the leg muscles are getting tighter, the back hurts more and Jin decides to go back and see Dave. He welcomes her in and listens once again to what she wants to achieve. Dave offers Jin a month's trial to see if they can work together and after the month is up he will decide if he wants to continue to work with her. This is a clever move as Jin wants him to want to continue with her journey. Jin sees Dave at his room where there are a dozen kettle bells, a mat, a box and some overhead bars. Not the usual gym set up at all.

One month later Jin has completed her trial period, she has lost a bit of weight and her legs are not pulling so much when she gets up from the floor. Dave offers to continue working with her (Goal one achieved) and Jin would like to carry on as she can see this is working.

The plan is to see Dave at his room every other week on a Friday and the other weeks they will speak on the phone. For 4 weeks this goes well, then Jin pulls her back and gets a cold. The exercises change to help the back and after a few weeks the strength returns in the legs, but Jin then realises, that in fairness, Dave can't see whether she is doing her daily exercises or not, she just needs to complete the app and thinks, "well as long as I do a few who will know."

We get to the start of month 3 and Dave and Jin meet at the room and Jin feels a complete burk as he can tell that she hadn't been doing enough of her exercises. She realises that whilst Dave holds her partly accountable, it is in fact Jin holding herself accountable that gets the results she is looking for.

Week two month three, Jin is actually doing all her exercises and feeling much better for it. When talking to Dave she tells him that this is what has happened to her and he replies that he could tell when the exercises were being completed properly and when a bit half-heartedly, but ultimately she needed to hold herself accountable to get the results that she wanted.

Month four we are now in Covid 19 lockdown part 2, exercises are being done properly, and the results are starting to be achieved. So how on earth can this strange little story help people in business?

Well I have been in business for many, many, many years and

I've seen highs and lows for my clients and I've had highs and lows in my business. The main thing that I have realised in the past few years is if I hold myself accountable to myself, my work and my clients then things don't get so stressed. Yes, we all have very busy times and quieter times, but you need to be true to yourself and hold yourself accountable for your actions. If you mess up don't beat yourself up, just admit it, fix it, try not to do it again, and move on.

www.silkbowgroup.com

Jen is a bookkeeper who loves great coffee and holidays in the sun. She has built her company reputation on being brutally honest.

/about Jen

O·N·L·E

fear/freedom/

/fear/freedom

PAUL HILL, HYPNOTHERAPIST & NLP PRACTITIONER.

/an exploration.

In these few paragraphs, I want to explore two powerful words - fear and freedom - not just in relation to their dictionary definitions, but in the way words and the emotion we attach to them affect us, as well as what their interplay means.

By way of example for the power of words:

'Stupid', according to Oxford Languages in Google, is 'having or showing a great lack of intelligence or common sense'.

'Silly' is 'having or showing a lack of common sense or judgement; absurd and foolish'.

Both similar in meaning, yet one has the ability to make us smile in its use, whilst frowning when using the other.

Think of something that really makes you smile, and as that smile spreads to its widest on your face, say the word 'stupid.' Not easy, Huh?

Repeat the process, except this time cause a frown with your thoughts. Just as your brows knit firmly together, say 'Silly'. Same issue?

We've attached such emotion to these two, small, everyday words as to make either one impossible to say while experiencing an emotion uncommonly associated with it.

Do the same with fear and freedom. You're right, there is no commonality, just test for emotion.

Say each word out loud then pause. What picture(s) come to mind? How do they make you feel? Is your tone when you say 'freedom' uplifting, whereas uttering 'fear' presses that tone down?

Freedom, as a word is buoyant, brings a smile, perhaps hope for better things. Fear, in and of itself, causes us to think of fearful things or to think fearfully. Changing the thought process requires practice; changing the language we employ is easy in comparison. Try different words like unease or apprehensive instead. Put them in a sentence. I fear spiders or I'm uneasy with spiders. I'm fearful of this job interview or I'm apprehensive of this job interview.

Make sense? Look out for other words you use which may cause a negative bias, google their synonyms and use them; I did.

Now let's explore the interplay.

Is it possible to live in fear of freedom? Can we live in fear and yet be free or are they mutually exclusive? Does freedom mean free of fear?

We often hear the term 'free from fear' as some sort of utopian ideal, but for now let's flip it and think about the 'fear of freedom'.

In discussing this topic in his book, 'No Time Like the Present: Finding Freedom, Love, and Joy Right Where You Are', Jack Kornfield quotes Jean-Paul Sartre as saying, "People often prefer a very limited, punishing regime rather than face the anxiety of freedom".

The anxiety of freedom stems from a fear of the unknown,

untried and untested. Surely not? I mean, you're free, aren't you? It's everyone's dream, isn't it? Try asking the many thousands of former Soviet Socialist Republic citizens, who having 'gained' their Western stylised freedom, yearn for a return to what they knew, tried and tested. Maybe for more than we realise, the freedom grass isn't so green?

In fear, can we be free? On his journey to rid India of the Colonial rule of the British Empire, Gandhi stated, "You can chain me, you can torture me, you can even destroy this body, but you will never imprison my mind". He suffered many physical attacks including at least eight separate attempts on his life, yet he had no fear in the face of death, believing that submitting to fear would be submitting to injustice upon himself. Gandhi demonstrated to the world that he wouldn't allow the spectre of fear to take a hold of his thoughts trusting, as he said, that "the future depends on what we do in the present".

When Mel Gibson, playing the Scottish outlaw William Wallace, cries, "freedom" as his entrails are being dragged from his living flesh, is his portrayal, albeit fictionalised, referring to and rallying his countrymen against their oppressor Edward I, or is he free in his own mind knowing that on his journey towards freeing Scotland, he has lived as a free thinking man? Perhaps his shout is a precursor to Gandhi's 'chain me' statement, above.

And so, can we be free from fear within freedom? Well I guess that's determined by your definition of freedom. Let's look at this popular western definition - freedom is the power or right to act, speak, or think as one wants without hindrance or restraint, and the absence of a despotic government.

Well the simple test is this, in referring to the above. Are you free? I believe we are, but only in so much as we aren't in fear of hindrance or restraint as detailed above, with a slight caveat. This freedom can be limited by laws that protect public safety.

The question isn't so much 'can we be free?' as 'do we want to be free?'. Yes, we want to be free from the fear of despotic rule etc., but fear isn't something to be feared for fear's sake. Fear triggers our fight or flight response which for millennia has been responsible for keeping us safe, in the most part. So far it's worked really well. I mean, we're still here. However, that response to danger hasn't modified in those millennia, and where we were justified in worrying about being eaten by a bear or fending off invaders in times gone by, we have no such justifications now. Yet we still have the same powerful, albeit outdated, fear and freedom response to the less devastating threats we encounter in our present.

In summary, words matter, a lot, as do definitions, but only dependent on the emotions we attach to them. Freedom is more likely to be found in the four inches between your ears than in some voted or fought for reality.

everydayhypnotherapy.com

Paul Hill, a hypnotherapist living and working in Southampton, using various techniques to passionately facilitate often life altering changes to clients' perspectives of themselves and the world they inhabit.

Carefully crafted language and positive affirmations form the solid foundation of a client centred practice.

/about Paul

**LAURA PAYNE-STANLEY,
TRUSTED ADVISOR & COACH.**

/want to play the fear freedom game?

We talk about fear and freedom frequently in everyday life, as though they are binary opposites. To be in fear is forgoing freedom and vice versa. That freedom is the ultimate place, the utopia of destinations for when we realise our human potential as business owners.

This false promise is a misnomer: it is one of a success mountain that has no top.

That to be seeking true freedom is never-ending and there is no finish line. But before we get into that, how did we get here in the first place? As business leaders and owners, how did we create a life and business that we are feeling a need to be free from?

To wind the clock back, as humans our main driver is based on pure survival.
It's primal, it's part of our DNA.

My story of becoming a serial entrepreneur started with this premise in mind: I need to survive so I started my own business. You may or may not resonate with this, and it may also apply to your own corporate or leadership life, securing roles that meant you survived or "should do" rather than those that enabled you to thrive.

In this construct of survival mode, we are constantly in a low level of fight or flight, which activates our sympathetic nervous system. In one essence this is wonderful for us, as the sabre tooth tiger isn't going to eat us because we are constantly on high alert. However, it also means that we are running in an induced focus of stress, which is exhausting.

If you are resonating with knowing that feeling of always being "on", of always being on alert mode and hustling, you will also know it becomes hard to sustain. So we seek out solutions to the symptoms of the problems that we are experiencing.

Overwhelm, burnout, anxiety, stress, depression, low libido, addiction and many more.

And I completely understand that your subconscious mind wants to remove or reduce the fear in you as soon as possible, so we seek out those easy solutions to the symptoms. Only for them to reappear at a later time.

Thus the cage of our own creation starts to be fortified. The bars and constraints that are holding us back seem to get thicker and more rigid. They become old friends. But what if true freedom can be when we dive deep into the fear of the problem that is creating those symptoms in the first place? So we can learn to drop the judgement of self and the war that arises internally between fear and freedom and embark on a quest of limitless potential.

What if we looked instead of not escaping the cage of our own creation, but that in our pursuit of true freedom we not only embrace the cage, but the fear that has previously kept the cage closed? At our innate core as humans we love to play. So if we look at our ability to "play" in the game of fear vs freedom, we can find pure peace in knowing the result upfront - that we will never win. For you are limitless and you are boundless, so the question becomes of your tolerance for fear response and freedom pleasure.

Let's imagine that the freedom that you desire, resides on the other side of your perceived level of tolerance to fear. And that the freedom that you desire to have, is contained within your hierarchy of aspiration, driven by what you conceive as being possible.

For when we have achieved the level of freedom that we desire, the mountain can move again because another human achieves another mountain top that becomes the summit for your new level of freedom.

Thus we are given the game of fear freedom. I invite you to join in and play.

The first rule of fear freedom: Make yourself uncomfortable.

As we now know that we need both elements of fear and freedom to participate in the game, you can't feel fear from within your comfort zone. To feel fear is to conceive of doing something uncomfortable.

So in business and in life, what is the task that you can do that you perceive will give you freedom, but that you feel a level of fear around?

Take action and do it. After all, 80% of success is showing up.

The second rule of fear freedom: Be a wannabe.

Part of the reason that your cage currently stands where it does, are the outer limits of aspiration or what you want to achieve.

When I was in infant school I wanted to be the Princess in Aladdin. I didn't get the role.
I created a cage of not being good on stage. This cage stayed until teenage years, when embracing the second rule

of fear freedom, I auditioned for National Youth Music Theatre. I didn't get in.

Continuing to embrace the second rule, I put myself in situations with leader speakers, experts, watched countless videos, trained and auditioned, always with the game of "Wannabe" in my mind.

The complex dynamic of playing the fear freedom game, wasn't a linear process, but fast forward, it took me from reserve lamp in Aladdin to TEDx official speaker.

This is my Fear Freedom Game story part 1. Now what is going to be your Fear Freedom success story?

Laura Payne-Stanley is an entrepreneur and frequent speaker on the topics of neuroscience, marketing and success.

www.trustelevatelabs.com

As a certified coach, Laura provides success support to entrepreneurs, visionaries and power couples to close the gap from where they are, to designing and creating a life they love and ongoing legacy.

Her clients include coaches, millionaire entrepreneurs, directors, elite athletes and couples.

/about Laura

PAM BATES,
SILKBOW GROUP.

/just say yes.

I have said 'YES' to many things, and boy how that took me to places and opportunities that set me up for life.

Have you ever been inspired by someone? I have. I met Major Kate Philip around 4 years ago. She is gracious, forthright, positive, courageous and someone I admire. I am privileged to be her friend. If you don't know the story, Major Kate lost a leg when an IED in Afghanistan took out most of her troop. With a prosthetic lower leg, she signed up for Walking with the Wounded charity along with Prince Harry to race to the South Pole.

My Real Inspiration.

However, my husband David, inspired me in every way. He encouraged me to set up an event company and model agency in the late 80's, and this was where my passion was ignited. Roll on a few more years, David opened the subject of buying a small place in Europe. Big mortgage in the UK, both working. I said, "Hell, yes, let's buy a house abroad."

The story starts with the idea of course. We had a five bedroom house and no savings (we spent a lot, especially with 4 children). I have already agreed to go with no misgivings, and if you want something, you can find ways to do it.

In August of 2001 we flew to Ancona in the Le Marche Region of Italy to check out what we could buy. Just a recce. After two days we made our way down to the Macerata province and had an hilarious time climbing in through windows of broken houses, being chased by wild dogs, encountering a huge barn owl - as I went in, he shot out. I'm not sure who was the most surprised. We were not really dressed for the job: me in a sarong and flip flops, and David with shorts, t shirt and flip flops. Obviously we were trudging through long grass and all sorts of wildlife, and to cap it all I trod on a snake who was enjoying sunbathing. I only realised when the estate agent screamed and ran away!

Day two was much better as we found a small town called San Ginesio, a medieval hill-top town with all its historic walls intact and four palaces. It was overlooking fields of poppies and sunflowers, with views across to the Sibillini Mountains. Later we drove up to Lake Fiastra fed by mountain streams. In winter it's filled with skiers and snowboarders.

I digress. The agents offered up the last house. We turned off the road onto a track and the best surprise was that it actually had a roof and windows. It had been abandoned for 30 years, but we fell in love with it. We asked the price and nearly fell over. This old farmhouse had three floors, 500 square metres with 2 hectares. Olive groves and all manner of fruit with wild asparagus. The price: forty two thousand pounds.

We said "yes".

We had found an amazing property but there was no electric, no water, no gas, no sewerage. Windows on the first and second floor but the lower floor used to be the cow shed and another part where they hung the hams etc. We flew home two days later and got the deposit sorted ready to go back at the end of October with friends, one of whom was an electrician. We should have looked at the weather. We knew it might be cold, but we were greeted with snow. Not much at the airport but when we got to San Ginesio, it was a skating ring, and getting through this medieval town was a challenge.

There's a whole story about the trip, but I'm writing a book.

However, just before Christmas I read in the local paper, that David's job was being advertised, and it stood out amongst the recruitment page. You can probably understand my first words when he walked into the house. His answer was, "ahh, I meant to tell you". His intention was to drive over in March 2002 to start tidying the land and do as much as he could before the builder started.

Our adventure in Italy was about to begin. We sold up in July, and finally, daughter Georgina (17) and I moved over in September 2002. So much for the holiday home, this was going to be a country house hotel and restaurant overlooking stunning mountains and a medieval town close by. Georgina was very influential as she spoke perfect Italian, and she is also good with people. We integrated with the Italians and shopped locally. I was privileged to be invited to take part in 'The Pallio', and we knew that we have been accepted.

David motivated everyone and it was pretty contagious. My 'let's say yes to everything' took me to places I would never have gone. We made a success of the hotel, although I still worked on events in the UK to boost the coffers while we were restoring.

If you can find someone who inspires and motivates you – keep them close.

Not the outcome we expected.

We had to go home after David been diagnosed with cancer. There were three operations in Italy and wonderful doctors, but we could not run the hotel so we returned to the UK in February 2011 to start again. I lost David to cancer in October 2011, and on the day of his funeral in the UK, all of the villagers gathered in our favourite restaurant in San Ginesio with the same reading in Italian before the church bells rang.

It took 2 years to sell our wonderful place, and the Euro had crashed just as David got the news of his cancer, so you can imagine, our hotel and business was valued before this at €800,000 euro. We finally sold for €210,000. As we owed taxes and utilities, I received £2000, and I managed to put a deposit on an Audi TT. I know that it may be strange, but we both loved sports cars and I know he would have approved.

To make some sense of losing him, I wanted to work for a cancer charity to use all of my connections over the years, and I believe I did a lot of good all round.

Just me

I hope in turn that I have inspired others to take on challenges in life through mentoring university students, entrepreneurs and business owners. It's a wonderful thing to encourage and inspire others.

We learnt so much along the way, but people were always in the back of our mind. Were we idiots to take this on? I don't regret anything that we did. You learn more from your mistakes. The outcome was obviously not what we wanted or expected, but the adventure I would do over again. David was my friend, love and inspiration. It really did come from him; it may sound a bit wet, but we always had something to share, and gave time to others.

I am drawn to those who have a passion for life, those who give freely and help others. The love of people can take you to do things you didn't think you could do. These are the people we need to listen to, how they react, how they make something from nothing – always with great ideas – they inspire me.

Have I had to be motivated by someone else? The answer is no. I love life and want to put the effort in for me. I don't need outside stimulus. I've been in business for over 40 years and done lots of different things, but what I do know is that people buy people. With that in mind, what is the difference between Inspiration and motivation? Both should give us a good feeling as one. Inspiration comes from inside you. Everyone and anyone can be inspired by thoughts, pictures, words, numbers. This is inventiveness, influence and bright ideas. Not necessarily original thought, but something exciting. I love to inspire people. It's one of the best things when I come up with something new or different, and something that I can share to help someone else.

When it comes to motivation, that's a slightly different thing, as motivation comes from within, motivation pushes you to act and take action. Stimulus, incitement to spur someone on. Motivation of course has many facets – for me it's about getting up in the morning and being happy and ready to take on another day. I don't need anyone to motivate me – it's a part of my makeup. Culture is everything, as without a common goal and shared values, how can we motivate and inspire? Coming together with others is the best human thing – so much can come out of one conversation, a moment in time, something or someone can change everything if you listen to yourself.

Who am I?

Throughout my life, I have taken risks – and this is because I was inspired by someone or something. My legacy will be to help others to make their own decisions, and to make the most of work-life. I love helping others, getting to know many people, and not just seeing them but finding out how they tick and how all of us can give our skills to encourage, inspire and motivate ourselves and others. This is a legacy. If all of us took notice of the person we're speaking to, and then for them to question themselves, how they can help others, then it's a job well done.

If you had your life again, what would you change? There have been so many opportunities within my lifetime. I feel privileged to have seen and heard everything from black and white TV to this incredible planet – not sure what will be my next great event.

To inspire and motivate is a very precious opportunity to help others. Why do I want to? I believe in people - the good, the bad, the ugly. Everyone has it in them to help others. Listen, listen, listen. Say yes. You won't know what you are missing if you don't.

www.silbowgroup.com

Pam Bates is an international event organiser. Mum to 4, Nanna to 9. FA referee. Said YES a lot.

Worked with the gliterati. Fast cars, super yachts, great food. Lived and worked in Le Marche, Italy for 10 years. Restored an abandoned farmhouse into a 9 bedroom country house hotel and restaurant.

/about Pam

**BETTY HEMINGWAY,
THE MINDSET ARCHITECT.**

/the power of stepping into conflict.

Conflict. Oh my, what a word, but as good a place to start as any.

Hit Google, and the definition from The Cambridge Dictionary states, 'an active disagreement between people with opposing opinions or principles'. Yet, the emotive reaction to the word conflict is huge. It seriously does not have a good rap. Its reputation precedes it in terms of negative perception, right? We can rename it, dress it up with a bow and give it another name, but the triggers and behaviours remain the same, so lets face it head on, with courage, curiosity and a metaphorical pair of learning lenses. Let us step into the conflict playground to explore how we can learn to find healthy resolution, not perceive it as a battle ground, and create better internal and external cohesion, together, in the workplace.

Why is the clatter of conflict so challenging?

Firstly, let's address why conflict has such a bad rap. In our early years, we may have seen arguments between parents, that led to emotions, reactions, fallout and even endings at home. Our private logic (individual psychology) in our sponge years means we would have absorbed the experience of conflict in our own way, and this impacts us of course in how we see conflict. When we look at the political landscape we see leaders standing firm, opposing opinions, with the volatile risk of disagreements; battle, risk, war, the win and lose effect, and the possible extreme outcomes that do harm. It can create the visual and emotional feelings of battle, of opening the wardrobe in the morning to put the shiny, cold metal armour on, picking up the shield of protection, and the weapon of choice.

What if I were to offer you a new viewing platform to experience the challenge of conflict with positive intentions? To simply tune in to understanding how you take part in the conversation, the impact, content, embracing differences and engaging in the possibilities of the resolution space together. Through developing your ability to suspend judgement, assumption and listen with intention and interest, you have the power to have engaging, energising growth opportunities where we explore differences without fear. What would it give you, your team, your organisation?

What if we were able to be more present in these types of conversations, with the ability to become more, not less receptive? What if you were able to recognise the part you create in the confronter or protagonist, and have the ability to take accountability, in the moment of disagreement? How would you feel? What if you were able to step away from the emotive prickly sharpness, or the need to win, and become part of a process of working through the conversation, like panning for gold?

As a Behavioural Leadership Coach, I have seen time and time again, when we apply ourselves, take ownership of our own behaviours, recognise what the reality is, verses 'story' or history (grudges) and look with a connective, we have the ability to surrender to change, and step towards a mutual space of understanding. Conflict can bring invaluable insight. It's about embracing the differences of opinion and not feeling threatened by, or disconnected form, the opportunity to find solution. I often ask, are you a contributor to the challenging conversation, or a detractor? When we allow the mind to not put up barriers, we have the freedom to listen to the perspectives of others, create new worlds, new ideas and ways of working, together. Let us start always from the position of you – what part do I play in this? Am I stepping into victim mode on the Drama Triangle, and if so, how does that trigger the Persecutor in the other person? Google the 'Dreaded Drama Triangle', and the 'Empowerment Triangle', my oh my, enjoy the read!

What part do we play?

Humans have the capacity to create bridges of shared curiosity that offers a kinder space to explore disagreements. To create an environment that offers a healthy space to work through problems, we need trust and rapport, connection, the ability to truly listen, curiosity, respect, and the ability to move on from the conflict.

My question is, what part do WE play in conflict? Is it conflict with self, conflict with others or our environment? How do we show up when we hear the cries of conflict? How do we react? Where does it come from? What is our relation to this internal reaction? What part of us shows up to do battle, and what is the impact of that in the workplace?

Let us start with you.

How do we work towards the greater good? When working with teams, I often draw on a myriad of psychologies and models, dependent on the needs of the organisation. I have a few favourites, and I wanted to share my fizzing admiration for their efforts in creating open spaces to share without fear, listen with depth, and allow our beautiful differences into the room.

I always lead with the word accountability. What part do you play here? How do you show up in conflict? What internal struggle do you have that projects and even distorts your perception of what is playing out in front of you? Our internal noise often affects out reactions, our triggers and then, our behaviours. This internal noise is referred to as your 'Internal orchestra' (sub personalities); critic, perfectionist, judge, cynic, protagonist, victim, rescuer, persecutor. Think of you as the conductor, and your orchestra around you. In conflict, do you think you are in a harmony or cacophony mode? Yup, the big base drum may be your reaction instrument, playing loud, taking over and disrupting your thinking process.

Gathering insight in the moment of the clatter – understanding the other side.

As humans, we tend to fall into five vessels as a reaction to conflict: compete, collaborate, accommodate, compromise, or avoid. If we can tune into the perspective of others in the moment of disagreement, we are able to show that we see value in the conversation, that the other is heard. This creates calmness, better flow and a 'downing of tools' so you can get to the heart of the problem faster.

With leaders and their teams, I offer new ways of interpreting, insight gathering if you will, through the three perspectives and the Gestalt chair. It goes like this. Three perspectives, position one, two and three. Position one is you: how you experience, what you hear and see, perceive, know and show up. We explore this in depth to understand things from YOUR perspective. I then ask the client to move to the second position, an empty chair. Here we explore position two: their perspective. You become that person, sharing their perspective, how they experience, view the world, the conversation, their frustration and so on. When we have gathered the gold from that seat, I ask the client to move to the third position. This is the balcony position: the overview, like looking down from a removed, dispassionate position, having seen these two positions play out. I ask specific questions, to stretch and challenge thinking, and allow the client to engage with how the differences and similarities look from this position. What is the gift in this conversation? Where is the alignment, what is the impact and what is the opportunity?

I believe, when we take accountability of our own responses, and open the door to step into a new thinking space, we can face confrontation with better mental limits, self-control, empathy, and a more receptive nature. If two people can do that, well, we have the opportunity to use conflict in a more positive way where we see someone has a passionate viewpoint. I lead my life with this one question: 'what is it?' Not as a negative, but a position of curiosity, openness, engagement, and awe. What would that give you? How would it nourish your conversations?

We cannot eradicate conflict. There is no delete button. It's about how we enter that space as participant. Be a contributor, make conflict a stepping stone to growth, don't make assumptions and try not to see barriers that are not there.

Albert Einstein said, "in the middle of difficulty lies opportunity." Essentially, the quality of our conversations within the disagreement space must start with understanding one another, listening, thinking about how we respond and seeing the opportunity of sharing transparency. Conflict is inevitable and there will always be differences of opinion, but in those moments, see it as a learning space, where there is mutual respect, and be curious. Remember, 'conflict cannot survive without your participation' (Wayne Dyer), so be the encourager, be the contributor, be the creator of positive influence. You've got this.

Betty Hemingway, The Mindset Architect, is a behavioural leadership coach with over 20 years experience of training, leading and coaching for change.

Coach, radio presenter and lecturer, she is an advocate for self accountability, transparency and discovery, offering a unique space to be curious, gather insight and get the breakthroughs for lasting change.

Using a blend of psychologies to get the deep work done, she offers a pair of metaphorical learning lenses to see things from a new perspective, creating the change necessary to thrive.

themindsetarchitect.co.uk

/about Betty

O·N·L·E

remote working/

/remote working

**DARREN NORTHEAST,
PR SPECIALIST.**

/developing and managing an e-culture in a digital environment.

As the very face of communications has changed beyond our imaginations in 2020, we are having to adapt our everyday lives. All without a plan, a training course or a manual. Little did we know as we entered 2020 that the very essence of how we communicate on a day to day basis was never going to be the same again.

Enter Zoom, Teams, WhatsApp groups and other online communication platforms. Very few of us had ever heard of them pre-lockdown, let alone used them – but here we are, and they have now become as important to our everyday lives as a mobile phone, PC and laptop. Working with these new communication platforms and learning how to use them, and use them effectively is one thing, but here is a whole different area that we need to work on and that is recreating a team culture via a laptop screen.

Seems virtually impossible, right?

With some creative thinking, we think this now opens up new opportunities when engaging a new culture across any team environment. So we can no longer meet over the office coffee machine, around the water cooler or feel part of the office community where a culture is developed, grown and embedded as part of our human touch points. So how can we grow and embed a new e-Culture across our teams via our new online communication channels?

An effective culture could start with a level of trust; trust in the new way we're working and fundamentally trust in each other and what we're doing. If we can feel trust in the organisation and our colleagues, we feel that this is great place to lay the foundations of developing a working culture for all. So this means having trusted processes in place. An example here would be regular online team meetings and everyone checking-in as to how they are feeling, what they're working on and what they've achieved, and if everyone is comfortable in doing so, this is then shared across the group to help with a feeling of attachment and support in the team.

Just because we are now mostly working online or remotely, working as a team is vitally important, so frequent and diarised meetings are essential, as it implies a routine for people to adhere to. People start to feel a little more comfortable emotionally in a routine and they know where they are and what's expected.

Providing emotional motivation to a team is vitally important (think of the scene from 'The Wolf Of Wall Street' where Warren Buffett is motivating his team). So, how can we do this virtually?

Our solution? Make it fun! Perhaps senior managers can provide a lunch and learn environment, whereby lunch could be delivered to the team via JustEat or using a local business to provide a delivered to your door working lunch. The emotional engagement that the team would have to the business would be worth every penny. So, they could attend a training session, or leadership presentation and be fed at the same time.

Encourage members of your team to go out and get away from the computer and laptop, and share their walks, exercise routines, fitness classes. Encourage the team to move. If this was a directive from the MD then people may feel more obliged to do it and encouraged to do so. But sharing of their motivations is key to this one, and ensuring the team are accountable for their exercise, movement, and well being. If the team has the fundamental elements of trust in place, then this could be encouraged to do during office and daylight hours. Just think how people will be empowered to get out and do something like this if they could do it during the working day.

No one is saying that an e-Culture can be developed overnight, or indeed the fact that what is put in place will be perfect from day one, so try things out and experiment, adapt, change and work with what is in place. And if it's not working, it's simple. Change it and try something else. Things like this need to be fluid and ever changing, and one size does not fit all!

Take away messages

- Have a routine in place - regular and diarised team meetings
- The way we communicate has now changed!
- Trust in the process, your team and your self is paramount
- Provide team motivation, but make it fun (and include food somehow!)
- Try developing an e-Culture – and if it's not working then change it!

www.darrennortheast.co.uk

Darren Northeast, the MD of Darren Northeast PR is a PR specialist running his own PR agency based in Bournemouth, Dorset.

Darren's agency has won a plethora of awards over the years, recognising their work in offering fully integrated PR campaigns to their client base from all over the UK.

/about Darren

O·N·L·E

GLEN LONG, FOUNDER,
EVOLVED BIZ.

/the questions.

One of my all-time favourite cartoon strips is one from Scott Adams, where Dilbert, the main character, asks his faithful pet Dogbert about the ethics of remote working. He wonders: "Do I owe my employer eight productive hours, or do I only need to match the two productive hours I would have in the office?"

It's very funny, and there's a truth at its heart: that working in an office isn't very productive. If you've worked in one for any length of time, you won't struggle to find examples of what I mean. Calendars filled with pointless meetings. Interruptions from strangely unbusy colleagues. Prolonged chats around the water cooler or inside the designated smoking area. The modern office witnessed the birth of presenteeism, where looking busy is more important than being busy, and being ambitious means arriving earlier and staying later than your boss.

In that environment, the challenge isn't how to get everything done in time, it's how to pass the time. As the end of the day approaches, you seem to slip into an Inception-like universe where minutes seem like hours.

In my first office job, our company moved floors and I have a clear memory of my colleagues and I waiting nervously for news of our desk allocation. The most prized spots in the open plan office were those in the corner, where nobody could see what was on your computer screen (giving you precious extra seconds to tap the "boss button" to switch Tetris for a convincing-looking Excel spreadsheet.)

Not long afterwards saw the arrival in the workplace of the

ultimate desk-based time-passer - the world wide web. (For anyone under forty, this was before Google was a verb, and when Yahoo and AltaVista reigned supreme.) I was always amused by those stories of employees being fired when their internet usage logs revealed they spent most of their days browsing non-work sites. I could never shake the idea that this was more embarrassing for their boss than for them. Shouldn't the lack of focus have been obvious in other ways?

More recently there was a story of the IT professional who outsourced his entire job to cheap overseas labour so he could spend the day working on personal projects. He was eventually caught and terminated by his employer for his behaviour and instantly hired by another for his ingenuity.

So if the average office isn't optimal for work, what about the average home?

The irony is that before the global pandemic, "working from home" (complete with air quotes) was often shorthand for goofing off or kicking back. It meant making yourself presentable above the waist for that one conference call of the day, then binge-watching Breaking Bad for the rest. Maybe that's why so many employers remained suspicious of remote working for so long. After all, when staff are out of sight, how can you be sure they're putting in the hours you're paying them for? In reality, the answer's simple. You focus on what they do, not where they do it.

I think this mental shift is long overdue. It turns out that remote working is the perfect antidote to presenteeism. When you can't judge someone by how visible they are in the office, you have to judge them on what they achieve, and isn't that really what work should be about? Getting sh*t done. Of course, that means thinking more carefully about what sh*t needs doing. Remembering why you hired someone in the first place and what a job well done actually looks like.

I've been working 100% remotely for over a decade and you'd have to drag me kicking and screaming back to an office, with its core hours, office politics and archaic expectations of daily tie-wearing. (God how I hated wearing a tie.)

My 9-to-5 is now a 10-til-1 then 2-til-3 then 4-til-8. Yes, my working day ends late, but by the time I wrap things up I can look back on a day where I've exercised, walked my dog (twice) and been there to greet my son as he walks through the door returning home from school.

My productivity is better than it ever was in an office. And on those days when it's not, that's on me. It's not because John from Accounts has stopped by to talk about Game of Thrones.

So is there nothing I miss about the old normal? I miss the office banter and the impromptu cake scrums that would form around the desk of the birthday boy or girl. But mostly it's what happened outside of the office that I miss. The evenings down the pub. The occasional off-site team-building jolly. I even have a strange nostalgia for the daily commute, although I suspect it would take less than a week of doing it again for that to evaporate.

In a post-pandemic world, many of the concerns about remote working will have disappeared. So will it stick? I think it will. In the short term many people will return to offices, but I think the contrast between "at home" and "at work" productivity will be stark. We've taken a bite from the apple and it'll be hard to forget the taste.

Longer term, the secret to making remote working work is doing a better job of recreating what's great about the real office in the virtual one. What's the virtual equivalent of a team lunch down the local pub? What's the best proxy for a birthday cake huddle? Likewise, how do we protect our home's status as a place to escape from work?

We don't have all the answers yet, but for me working remotely brings opportunities to do business as fully-rounded humans. Escaping the office offers a new type of freedom. And I don't just mean the freedom to work in your underwear.

www.evolved.biz

Glen Long has been helping businesses harness internet technologies since the mid-1990s, when few people knew what a URL was, let alone had one. Today he's the founder of Evolved Biz, helping small business owners create more time, money and impact by packaging their know-how as engaging online courses.

/about Glen

JON BAKER,
THE INTROVERT IN BUSINESS.

/the work from home problem.

Every business is a collection of humans (stakeholders in management speak) working together to create something. Probably a product or service which creates cash. That could be a one-person business where the owner deals with customers, suppliers and others, or a traditional large business with many staff.

Where people work together, some form of focus normally makes work more effective. Rarely do a group of people work together with no focus and make stuff effectively.

You might call it organisation, control, management, or just focus. This focus can make business worse, or better, for humans. Creating human focus is harder where people work in different places.

The infamous meeting

Saying, "let's have a meeting", makes most people groan inwardly, but creating focus in a group involves some sort of meeting. This article explores what's going wrong to make meetings so bad and some tips on how making business better for humans can improve the effectiveness of these meetings.

The challenges of home and hybrid working.

Creating focus is easier when all the people are in one place (an office). It's easier to control, coordinate and possibly be creative. Working from home can allow greater freedom for staff, but make it harder to coordinate, control and act together. Factions and office politics create tension and reduce focus. They normally exist where some people are "in the know" and others not. It's less likely if everybody is in the same office. When working from home that can be harder, making factions more problematic.

But when some people work in the office, some at home, and some switching between both, additional factions occur ("she isn't up to date as she's only working from home", "he isn't working as hard, as he's in the office and spending more time chatting" etc.).

We are all different and we're all the same

We all want to achieve something meaningful from our work and want to be treated as human beings, in line with our values. There sits the problem. Our values normally vary and what we want from work varies, so we all want different things. Good business takes these different views into account and is stronger for it. Home working en-masse and the development of permanent hybrid working patterns make this harder.

Different personality types

Understanding different types of personality can help improve communications. A simple method is to consider the difference between introvert and extrovert.

- **Extrovert:** Tend to enjoy being in a group of people and struggle more when working alone. Extroverts tend to "talk to think", in other words, asked a question their immediate verbal responses are part of their thinking process. So, they're often happy in busy meetings where the style is "brainstorming" or calling out impromptu answers.

- **Introvert:** Tend to feel more tired when in a group of people and recover that energy when alone.They tend to "think to talk", which can give more coherent, complete, and detailed answers, but lead to a short delay before answering. So, introverts may not perform at their best when "put on the spot" in a group setting, meaning impromptu calling out doesn't put them at their best.

- **Ambivert:** This group comprises different levels of introvert and/or extrovert. They can therefore have the advantages, and disadvantages, of both categories. What's the best sort of meeting for them? Contemplative or brainstorming? It depends on where the person is on the introvert/extrovert scale.

Meetings are about creating focus

Meetings in business, when run well, create focus (control). Where they run badly it's either because they're about somebody exerting power, or because the attempt at creating focus isn't working. This leads to the normal reaction to the idea of having a meeting - "what a waste of time" and sayings like "a camel is a horse designed by committee". We may not be good at running office meetings, but at least we're all in the same place, know what to expect, can interact seamlessly and the meeting can extend past the meeting's end as the team congregate and chat afterwards. Hybrid meetings (some in the office and some at home) add complexity. Some people get the benefits of office meetings and others don't.

Making business more human

So, we can't escape meetings, nor the fact that people have different requirements. Making business better for humans, and more efficient, needs better meetings which take into account differing needs of introverts, extroverts, and everybody in between.

Tips for improving meetings, however they're held.

1. **Collaborative agenda:** Getting everybody involved in the meeting is a good way to allow different views into the room, and for business to be better for humans, especially in online meetings. Using online documents or polls to see what's most important can create a more effective agenda.

2. **Use the agenda:** One of the most hated meeting issues is where they drag on and get lost, although one person's "drag on" may be another person's "perfect time". Keeping to the agenda allows everybody to know where you are and reduces human dropout, especially in online meetings.

3. **Give the gift of time:** The difference between people who "talk to think" and "think to talk" means there can be a time versus detail pressure. Anything that allows extra time for processing thoughts reduces this. Introverts tend to "think to talk". Putting them on the spot doesn't make them effective, or feel comfortable. Getting the agenda out early, along with all of the data that you're going to discuss in a meeting, will allow them to engage more in the meeting as they're able to process their thoughts in advance. You never know, even some of the extroverts may read it early - a win all round.

4. **Hold back:** When you want the quieter ones in the meeting to speak up more, you need to get the louder ones to hold back. That could be by time limiting everybody, or simply being stronger at stopping some people from talking. Most extroverts don't take exception to this, when done politely, if they know their main point was heard. So, cut in, summarise their main point and

move on to somebody else.

5. **Write it:** Ring the changes and have meetings where everybody is not allowed to call out whatever they first thought of. No more brainstorming. Your meeting will be more human, for more people, as a result. Try brainwriting, use the chat box, use online polls, wordclouds, or simply get everybody to silently write their answer on paper for two minutes before each reads out their thoughts. This allows more people to process their thoughts and air their views. Your meeting will be more effective as a result and it will feel more human for more people.

Making business more human

A modern mixture of hybrid working from office and home creates stresses for people and challenges for keeping the business focused. Although everybody hates meetings, the answer is more meetings. But these meetings need to consider personality types, be shorter, more engaging, more focused, and more effective. Some more focus on the quieter introverts in the team will help to achieve those aims.

introvertinbusiness.co.uk

Driven by his desire to expose the talent of quieter business people, with his enthusiasm for action and helping others, Jon Baker has become known for inspiring business leaders into action.

With his quietly confident attitude to challenges and vision of balanced teams, Jon Baker has become known for activating introverts.

/about Jon

O·N·L·E

Book a meeting today.

www.theonle.network

Printed in Great Britain
by Amazon

66036179R00093